DESTINY

IN THE

PALM

OF YOUR

HAND

DESTINY
IN THE
PALM
OF YOUR
HAND

CREATING YOUR FUTURE
THROUGH VEDIC
PALMISTRY

Ghanshyam Singh Birla

Destiny Books
Rochester, Vermont

Destiny Books
One Park Street
Rochester, Vermont 05767
www.InnerTraditions.com

Destiny Books is a division of Inner Traditions International

Library of Congress Cataloging-in-Publication Data

Birla, Ghanshyam Singh.
    Destiny in the palm of your hand : creating your future through Vedic
palmistry / Ghanshyam Singh Birla.
        p. cm.
    Includes index.
    ISBN 0-89281-770-4
    1. Palmistry. I. Title.

BF921 .B57 2000
133.6—dc21

                                         00-022654

Printed and bound in Canada

10 9 8 7 6 5 4 3 2 1

Text design and layout by Virginia L. Scott-Bowman
This book was typeset in Goudy

This book is dedicated to my beloved Gurudev Paramahansa Yoganandaji,
whose teachings strengthened my faith in the importance of
self-analysis to harmonize body, mind, and soul.

Man's purpose is complete freedom from unhappiness.

Swami Sri Yukteswar

Acknowledgments

It is with a great sense of privilege and joy that I present to my readers *Destiny in the Palm of Your Hand*, an introduction to the ancient art and science of Vedic palmistry.

First and foremost I would like to thank my long-time senior students, friends and fellow morphologists, Kathleen Keogh, vice-president of The Palmistry Center, and her brother, Peter Keogh, director of my country retreat, for their dedication in helping me materialize this book under the chief editorial guidance of Patricia Munro Conway to whom I am truly indebted.

I also sincerely thank my colleague and friend Guylaine Vallée, for the long hours she spent in compiling the material for this book; Sophie Bisaillon for her beautiful artwork; Nazneen Wallis for editing these pages from beginning to end; my beloved son Keero for his excellent graphic design, along with Johanne Riopel, who is also responsible for bringing my first book *Love in the Palm of Your Hand* to the French audience.

Sincerest gratitude to Chandan Rugenius for his Ayurvedic massage; Denise Parisé and Jacinthe Côté and Rémi Riverin for "holding the fort"; Marie-Claire Sauvé for her organizational work; Grace Macklin for her transcribing zeal; my loving wife Chanchala along with Heather Flockhart for their delicious vegetarian cuisine; my beautiful daughter Rekha and my loving son Abhishekananda for their vigilant watch on meeting deadlines; and my love and gratitude to all my friends, staff, and volunteers—Élyise Trépanier, Hélène Bergeron, Jacqueline Poirier, Huguette Allen, Francis Desjardins, Mary Stark, Pasquali Roberto, and Geeta Sharma, M.D. Thanks to Tania Desjardins, physicist, for her insights into the microcosmic world of the universe. Thanks also to Colette Hemlin for her contribution to the "Magnetic Pen" along with Mil Winter for their eleventh hour rescue.

I am especially grateful to Dr. David Frawley, a modern sage of Jyotish for his insightful and enlightening foreword. I am also grateful to my friend and colleague, Dr. A.K. Bhattacharya, who continues to ignite my heart with his loving inspiration.

Thanks to my publisher and all the staff of Inner Traditions for their support and kindness— Ehud Sperling as publisher, Deborah Kimbell (associate publisher), Jon Graham, (acquisitions editor), Laura Schlivek (project editor), Cannon Labrie (copy editor), Peri Champine (art director), Ginny Scott (designer), Priscilla Baker (typesetter), Jeff Euber (publicist), Andy Sak (sales), Cynthia Fowles (international rights). We would also like to take this opportunity to thank Mary Elder Jacobsen for her work on *Love in the Palm of Your Hand*, which helped in the creation of this subsequent book in the series. Special thanks to Kristi Tate and Susann Cobb for their care and hospitality at my book signing at The Natural Products Expo East in Baltimore. Much gratitude to Dr. Vatsala Sperling for her inspired and beautiful cover rendition of the story of Kalidas. Lastly, thanks to all my clients, students, friends, and family who allowed me to use their hands for my research over the last several decades, which has culminated in this series of books.

Contents

Foreword

Perhaps nowhere in the world is palmistry better developed than in India, the ancient land of spirituality and mysticism. It is an integral part of the disciplines of yoga and meditation that have always characterized Indian culture. Vedic palmistry, the palmistry of India, is a subtle art and science that explores the many mysteries of our karma and destiny. It is based on the principles of the Vedas, ancient yogic scriptures that bring the wisdom of great sages to bear on the secrets of the conscious universe in which we live. Vedic palmistry reveals the inner needs and purposes of our souls, while at the same time it points to specific events in our outer lives.

In India palmistry is used along with astrology. When one says that one practices Jyotish (which means astrology), people immediately show you their palms. Vedic palmistry and Vedic astrology are intimately related. The Vedic system reveals a remarkable correlation between the hand and the birth chart. The palm shows the strength or weakness of planets similar to those indicated by the positions in the birth chart. The hand, like the chart, indicates the life experience of a person as well as the remedial measures a person should take to balance or improve his or her planetary influences. Through looking at both the palm and the birth chart, one gains a twofold perspective. The process is like crossing horizontal and vertical lines to pinpoint exactly what is occurring in one's life.

Vedic astrology is rapidly gaining popularity in the Western world and is now recognized as one of the most accurate and profound astrological systems available today. It contains many more calculations and considerations than the usual Western astrology, including twenty-seven lunar mansions (*nakshatras*) and a complex system of planetary periods (*dashas*), which gives it a unique place among astrological systems. As the current president of the American Council of Vedic Astrology (ACVA), I have watched interest in this subject grow steadily. While Vedic astrology was once an obscure rarity in this country, it is now a major movement in astrological circles. Vedic astrology provides insight into all domains of life including career, relationships, finances, spirituality, and mental and physical health. Vedic palmistry has the same range of applications and can serve as a comprehensive guide for self-realization. In a few years we have seen our Vedic astrology organization grow from a few scattered individuals to nearly five hundred people. In the course of our various programs and conferences we have invited many teachers to speak on Vedic astrology, including a number from India. It was in this context, in February 2000, that I first met Ghanshyam Birla when he spoke at our Seventh International Symposium on Vedic Astrology in Sedona, Arizona. Ghanshyam took the time to look at my palm along with both the hora chart (chart for the moment) and my birth chart. He made several important and accurate observations about my life and destiny. Above all, he was able to communicate his insights with clarity and consistency, both relative to the facts of the palm and the chart and relative to the movement of my outer and inner lives. He demonstrated a remarkable command of his subject, a methodical approach, and the ability to make what he saw relevant on a spiritual level.

Ghanshyam Birla is one of India's and the world's foremost palmists and astrologers, with many years of experience in the East and the West. He combines palmistry and astrology together in his readings, following the venerable Vedic tradition, a tradition that he has been thoroughly trained in since childhood. He is well aware of the spiritual potential of each person and the yogic paths each should follow to promote his or her inner evolution. At the same time he is aware of each person's human needs and karmic compulsions; these aspects cannot be ignored and must be fulfilled before an individual can go beyond them. Ghanshyam is no mere fortune-teller but a wise counselor and guide who wants the best for his clients and is able to enter into a deep and lasting rapport with them. *Destiny in the Palm of Your Hand* is not his first book but is one of many. It is the second of a trilogy on palmistry, and shows his great skills as an author. No other writer in the West presents Vedic palmistry with such depth of detail, while at the same time conveying the information in such a clear and understandable manner. The hand is a mirror of our soul and Ghanshyam Birla shows us how to access this mirror without distortion. The book is well organized, almost like a course on the subject, and leads its reader step by step to a practical understanding of its arcane topic. It contains important illustrations and remarkable stories that serve to drive home the author's points, making them relevant on a personal level. Most notably, Ghanshyam shows that palmistry is a dynamic art, part of the movement of life both within and without. For him the hand reveals not merely the fixed karma of the past but our positive vitality that can serve to shape our personal future as well. Our destiny is not some heavy weight that we have to carry around like a ball and chain, rather it is a creative force that we can channel to fulfill our deeper aspirations for ourselves and for humanity and the world as a whole. The lines on the hand do change over time and we can work consciously to help them change in a positive direction. Ghanshyam provides a comprehensive and integral strategy for positively managing our destiny. In this way his approach to palmistry is very different from the dire predictions associated with palm reading. His analysis of the palm becomes a liberating factor that can be integrated into any personal strategy for self-realization. He removes palmistry from the realm of mere fortune-telling and places it solidly into the field of holistic healing, where it can be used as a tool for enhancing life at all levels. Ghanshyam's book contains a remarkable explication of the Vedic and yogic disciplines that culminate in palmistry and astrology. He shows how yoga, palmistry, and astrology relate to one another and how they can be used together to plot our journey back to God, our true Self. One is struck by his simplicity and clarity of expression. Ghanshyam's book is like a breath of fresh air compared to the many confusing and poorly written books from India on Indian spiritual disciplines. He saves the reader from wading through numerous such texts to find a few gems of wisdom. Instead, he places all the gems of Vedic palmistry in the palm of your hand.

Dr. David Frawley (Vamadeva Shastri)
President, American Council of Vedic Astrology (ACVA)
Author of *Astrology of the Seers, Yoga and Ayurveda*, and
Ayurvedic Healing—A Comprehensive Guide

Introduction

This book is the second in a series of themes in palmistry. The first book, *Love in the Palm of Your Hand,* deals mainly with how to develop loving relationships and how by beginning with ourselves and our own magnetism we are able to attract better circumstances into our lives and help enhance the ones that are already there. This book, *Destiny in the Palm of Your Hand,* explains the Vedic view of how we manifested from infinite spirit and how we can bring that unlimited creative vision into our lives. *Destiny in the Palm of Your Hand* looks into the more esoteric aspects of palmistry that relate to how our past patterns can affect our future destiny. This book will explore those patterns and their meanings and discuss how we can turn our life around and re-create our future as well as atone for any mistakes of the past. If we can change those patterns ultimately our future destiny lies in the palms of our hands.

THE HANDS—OUR PERSONAL SIGNATURE

We all know that no two fingerprints are identical, but in fact, the entire hand is unique in its pattern of lines. The lines are unique precisely because each of us has personal memories, hopes, and individual character traits. Since there is a traceable link between our personality, thoughts, and experiences and the way the lines form on our hands, our handprints represent a kind of personalized signature.

THE LINES CHANGE

Just as we continue to change and evolve, so do the lines on our hands. As our personality matures, our attitudes, priorities, activities, and companions may also change. These important changes are all reflected in the hand. A study of our hands provides us with a method of analyzing ourselves objectively, which allows us to make more positive choices regarding our work, our dealings with people around us, and many other important aspects of life. We will find ourselves less likely to repeat or perpetuate mistakes. With time, the improvements we make in our lives will register on our hands.

PREVENTION VERSUS PREDICTION

Palmistry is associated in the minds of many people with the notion of prediction. This idea comes from an incomplete understanding of palmistry.

We all have predispositions toward certain kinds of behavior. For example, if someone we loved betrayed our trust when we were young, we may have difficulty being open to finding a loving partner. A study of the lines and signs on our hands can show us the patterns we have developed in response to past hurts. Unless we take positive steps to change, we will continue to perpetuate the patterns.

By learning to understand the significance of the lines and signs on our hands as indicators of predispositions we can decipher trends in our behavior. An experienced analyst can suggest the likelihood of future behavior and events. Armed with this information, we have the freedom both to confirm and nurture our strengths and potentials and to decide what changes we wish to make in our lives.

Much of the fun in studying palmistry comes from seeing how we can exercise our free will in more informed and effective ways. Each time we take a new direction in our lives, we are able to see corresponding changes in the lines and signs on our hands. No two palm readings will, therefore, be identical. A professional palmist can best assist his or her clients by pointing out precisely how past and present thoughts and actions have set each of them on a certain course. With guidance, effort, and patience, we can improve in attitude and behavior. As our

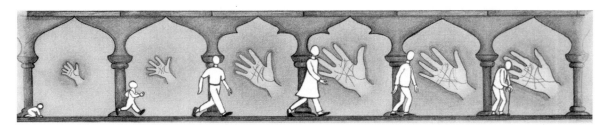

Just as we continue to change and evolve, so do the lines on our hands.

thinking changes and new behavior patterns become familiar, the lines and signs and even the mounts (the underlying tissue of the hand) will undergo detectable changes. Even lines indicating future trends can change: Broken lines can be mended; lines showing interferences and obstacles can fade and disappear; lines showing positive associations and relationships can appear, and so on. Admittedly, deeply ingrained major lines indicating entrenched tendencies in our subconscious are slower and more resistant to change. Nevertheless, these too can respond with patient effort.

Examples Illustrating How the Lines Change

Larry was successfully working in the entertainment business performing as a clown at parties. Increasing demands encouraged him to develop his own business. The pressure of performing in public, however, made him more and more anxious. His lifestyle was reflected in his "before" print by a busy network of crisscrossing lines. His "after" print shows the same person eighteen months later. During this time Larry found success in his own business, practiced yoga and meditation, and in the process gained a new outlook on life. The pattern of lines on his hands shows less stress, reflecting his new lifestyle.

Ivan's first handprint was taken when he was attending college. At that time he was confused and lacked direction. Ivan eventually went on to complete his Ph.D. in religious studies. This is shown by improvements in the features evident in the later handprint.

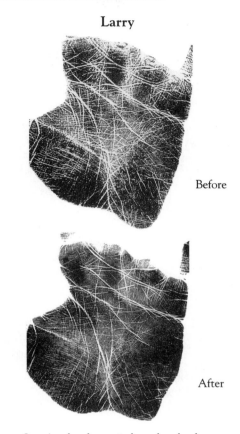

Larry

Before

After

Larry's reduced stress is shown by a less busy network of crisscrossing lines in his "after" handprint.

Marcel is a retired sales representative. After concentrating for many years on the practical concerns of business and family life, he found retirement a wonderful opportunity to explore his creative, inventive side. He enrolled in painting and sculpture courses at his local arts center. His head line and Mercury line reflect these changes in his "before" and "after" handprints.

These cases illustrate that our destiny is not carved in stone. We can take active steps to improve our lives once we have gained better self-understanding. We can help ourselves and others to understand the past, deal with the

Ivan

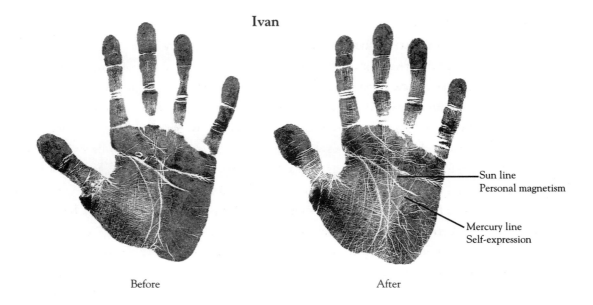

Sun line
Personal magnetism

Mercury line
Self-expression

Before

After

Ivan's ability to communicate better is confirmed by the line of Mercury—the line of self-expression—named after Mercury,
the winged messenger of the gods. Also note the appearance of the Sun line,
which denotes greater personal magnetism.

Marcel

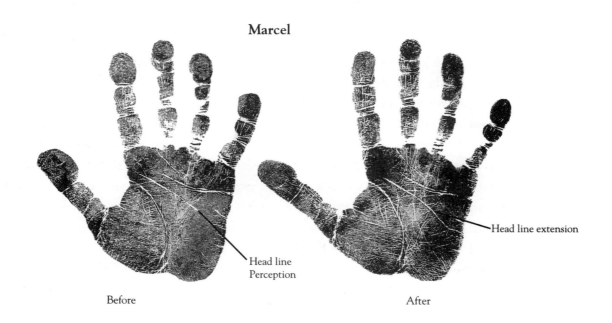

Head line extension

Head line
Perception

Before

After

Note the extension of Marcel's head line in the "after" handprint, reflecting greater optimism
and belief in his capabilities.

present, and mold the future in such a way as to bring forth the best qualities of heart, mind, and soul. This is the challenge and also the reward of undertaking a serious study of palmistry.

The Story of Kalidas

Once upon a time, there was a young princess known throughout the kingdom for her brilliance. As she was approaching the age when she should marry, some vindictive and cruel courtiers plotted to trick her by finding the most ignorant man in all the kingdom to be her husband.

The courtiers searched throughout the land, and, in time, they came upon a peasant sawing a branch off a tree. He was sitting on the limb he was sawing, but on the side that was about to fall. In addition, he was directly above a deep well. The courtiers were overjoyed. "Here is the ideal match for our princess!"

"Sir," they cried in unison, "please come down from your perch. You are about to do serious damage to yourself." They had no intention of losing their perfect candidate for the princess's hand.

After careful preparations designed to convince the princess of her suitor's worth, the young man, named Kalidas, was presented to her. After a short engagement, they were married. Soon afterwards, the princess found that Kalidas wasn't all that she had believed him to be. She was desperately disappointed by their inability to communicate with each other. "We will not speak again," she told him, "until you have learned to communicate in Sanskrit to my satisfaction."

Kalidas, a complete illiterate, returned to the tree where he was first discovered by the scheming courtiers, sad, dejected, and confused. He looked up and saw the partially sawn branch still clinging to the trunk of the tree. He looked down and saw the gaping mouth of the well directly below it. He realized then how foolish he had been. Sinking to his knees by the side of the well, he began to weep. How would he ever begin to satisfy the impossible demands of his new bride?

Through his tears, he saw a woman lowering an empty jug into the well by a rope. As she raised the jug, the rope slid into a well-worn groove. Wiping his eyes, he realized that the groove had been cut deep into the stone by thousands of ropes that, likewise, had been used to pull water from the depths of the well. If a rope could cut into stone, he thought, perhaps he could also establish new grooves in his patterns of thinking. Encouraged, he began to study. In time, he became a learned scholar and the author of the *Abhijyan Shakuntalam*, one of the most revered classics of Sanskrit literature. Eventually, he won the heart of his wife.

This story is a great example of how, by determined efforts, we can change our destiny. Now let us turn our attention to the steps we can take to bring about positive changes.

SEVEN STEPS TO MANAGING OUR DESTINY

No matter what tendencies we have, we need not be affected by them throughout our whole life. We have the free will to change.

What steps can we take to bring about positive changes? We must be patient and diligent. It takes time before a conscious mode of behavior filters through into our subconscious and becomes automatic. By understanding the implications of the following sequence of steps, we can teach ourselves to exercise our free will constructively.

Breath

It is our breathing that gives birth to our thoughts. We need our breath, which sustains our lives, to transform an idea into living reality. When we learn to control the quality and depth of our breathing, we channel our life force, or *prana*—a subtle form of breath responsible for giving us strength and energy.

Thought

Deep, balanced breathing—when the cycle of inhalation and exhalation is effortless—creates a state of inner calm in which clear, objective thinking can occur. We become more focused on the present moment without losing sight of the greater context.

Action

Once we are able to think clearly about a situation or problem, we will know how to act. We will be able to discriminate between what we want and what we need. We will be able to determine what is really good for us and what is not.

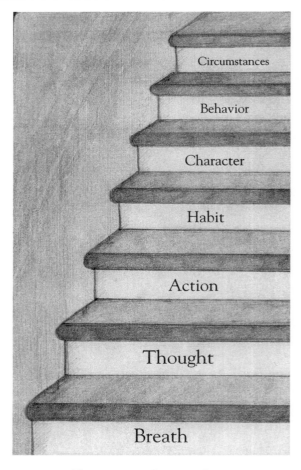

The seven steps to harmonious living.

Habit

When we practice positive patterns of behavior, we create habits. While these new actions may require conscious effort at first, over time they become second nature.

Character

Habits provide the foundation of our character. Once a series of desirable repeated actions becomes an unconscious habit, we realize that we have begun to change our past tendencies.

Behavior

Our behavior reflects the changes in our inner nature, our character. Others perceive us as wiser and more loving.

Circumstances

With a more positive attitude and behavior, we find that the circumstances of our lives will improve. We find greater harmony in our work, in our personal relationships, and in our spiritual life.

THE IMPORTANCE OF YOGIC BREATHING IN VEDIC PALMISTRY

Proper breathing is the foundation for changes in attitude and behavior, which in turn allow us to attract positive circumstances into our lives. Yogic tradition places great emphasis on the technique of breathing so that we can achieve a balance between incoming and outgoing—or cool and warm—breaths, establishing a neutral zone. Ideally, the incoming breath should equal the outgoing breath in depth and duration. This produces a balance between cool (incoming) and warm (outgoing) breathing that results in a neutral state. The life force or *prana* (referred to as *chi* in Chinese and *ki* in Japanese) can now flow without impediment.

Most of us recognize the benefit of taking a few deep breaths when we are anxious, stressed, or in pain. By breathing deeply we are cooling down our overstimulated emotions. We are also giving our intellect an opportunity to distance us from the source of our unease. Similarly, we often sigh or exhale forcibly in response to sorrow, anger, or frustration. In the process we are letting off steam, releasing an overabundance of heat. We are attempting to bring our feelings into balance with our mind. In both instances, there is a conscious effort to reach a balance between our emotions and our reason.

Once we learn to balance our breath, we can create a proper environment in which positive changes can occur. As we have seen, with time, these changes are reflected in the lines and signs of the hand.

1
Vedic Palmistry

The earliest Hindu sacred writings, known as the Vedas, consist of collections of hymns, prayers, and liturgical formulas as well as teachings on ultimate reality and the liberation of the soul. The word *veda* means "knowledge" in Sanskrit.

Vedic palmistry is the study of the structure and markings of the human hand. The ancient *rishis*, or seers, believed that there was a correlation between the visible features of the hand, the conscious mind, subconscious thought processes, and the

The classic, golden age of palmistry dates back to the Vedas, India's most sacred texts.

8

superconscious intuition of spirit. The study of Vedic palmistry provides a language for expressing this body/mind/soul connection. Its purpose is to help us gain self-understanding.

The interpretation of the data available to us in the hand enables us to see where our hidden potentials lie. We can learn to resolve inner conflicts by establishing an equilibrium in body, mind, and spirit. By eliminating self-defeating attitudes, we can harness our inner resources.

We can apply what we learn about ourselves through the study of palmistry to specific areas of daily life: career guidance, health diagnosis, marital counseling, interpersonal conflict resolution, and spiritual direction.

THE GOLDEN AGE OF PALMISTRY

The golden age of palmistry as a spiritual science began in India about 5,000 years ago with the Vedas. There are four books of these sacred writings: the Rig, Yajur, Sam, and Atharva Vedas. Sri Aurobindo, a great Indian master and scholar of Vedic thought, explains the origin of the Vedas as follows: "The language of the Vedas itself is *sruti*, a rhythm not composed by the intellect but heard, a divine word that came vibrating out of the infinite to the inner audience of the man who had previously made himself fit for the impersonal knowledge."*

*Harvey P. Alper, *Mantra* (Albany, N.Y.: State University of New York Press, 1989), 165.

Around 800 B.C., in order to make the Vedas more accessible to humanity, the ancient seers compiled and translated them into six ancillary branches of knowledge that were referred to as the Vedangas. The Vedangas, literally "limbs" of the Vedas, comprise the cosmic individual, the Ved Purusha. The six branches or limbs are: *shikksha* (phonetics), *kalpa* (rituals), *vyakaran* (grammar), *nirukta* (etymology), *chhandas* (meter), and *jyotish* (knowledge of heavenly bodies). *Jyotish*, which represents the "eyes" of the Vedas, translates as "Lord of Light"—from the Sanskrit root *jyot*, meaning "light." (It is interesting to note that the word *jyo* itself means "to advise.")

Jyotish, then, is the study of the effects of light on human beings. Therefore, it refers to astronomy, the science of the movements of the heavenly bodies, and astrology, the study of the influence of the planets on our lives. The *rishis* and priests of India depended on these sciences, as Vedic rituals were more effective when performed at auspicious times, that is, under the influence of particular constellations. Later, the belief developed that not only Vedic rituals but all aspects of human endeavor, both individual and communal, were affected by the planetary bodies. Thus, after extensive research, the science of astrology was developed. The two sciences of *nakshatra vijyan* (or astronomy) and *phalit jyotish* (predictive astrology) together came to be known as *jyotish*.

The literature devoted to the science of *jyotish* can be divided into a number of fields of study, each of which complements the others.

Their common focus was the investigation of how large-scale changes in the energy patterns of the macrocosm—for example, changes in the planets and constellations—have directly traceable effects upon the smaller scale of the microcosm, most particularly at the level of human life. An understanding of these sciences allows us to exercise our free will either to enhance positive effects or to minimize negative ones.

One of the branches of *jyotish* is *samhita shastra*, the mathematical knowledge that deals with choosing auspicious times for particular events. For example, certain constellations are good for marriage, studying, planting, and harvesting. Others are appropriate for meditation, making an important purchase, signing a contract, and so on.

From *samhita* came *angvidya*, the study of the various body parts in relation to planetary stimuli. From this branch came the field of *samudrik shastra*, which translates as "the ocean of knowledge." *Samudrik shastra* interprets all features of the human body, including the size, shape, color, texture, lines, signs, and markings, as indicators of trends in personality and behavior. *Samudrik shastra* is divided into three parts: *mukh shastra*, the study of the lines, signs, and markings of the human face; *paad shastra*, the study of the lines, signs, and markings on the feet; and *hast rekha shastra*, the study of the lines, signs, and markings on the hands, known as palmistry.

The writings devoted specifically to the exploration of the human hand are collectively known in Sanskrit as *hast jyotish*, which translates literally as "the science of hand analysis." As we have seen, the purpose of *hast jyotish* is primarily preventive rather than predictive.

Now let us turn our attention to one of the underlying concepts of Indian philosophy. The *rishis* taught that the universe has organization and structure; it is not a random, meaningless construct. Throughout creation, there is an observable pattern that manifests itself from the largest galaxy to the tiniest atom.

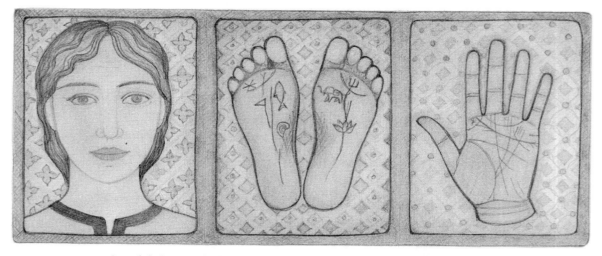

Samudrik shastra is divided into three parts: the study of the human face, feet, and hands.

The Vedic Roots of Palmistry

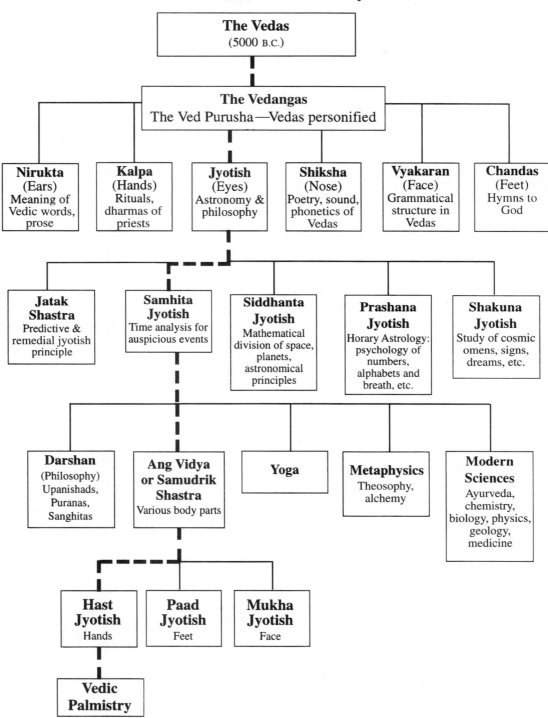

The Vedas
(5000 B.C.)

The Vedangas
The Ved Purusha—Vedas personified

Nirukta
(Ears)
Meaning of
Vedic words,
prose

Kalpa
(Hands)
Rituals,
dharmas of
priests

Jyotish
(Eyes)
Astronomy &
philosophy

Shiksha
(Nose)
Poetry, sound,
phonetics of
Vedas

Vyakaran
(Face)
Grammatical
structure in
Vedas

Chandas
(Feet)
Hymns to
God

**Jatak
Shastra**
Predictive &
remedial jyotish
principle

**Samhita
Jyotish**
Time analysis for
auspicious events

**Siddhanta
Jyotish**
Mathematical
division of space,
planets,
astronomical
principles

**Prashana
Jyotish**
Horary Astrology:
psychology of
numbers,
alphabets and
breath, etc.

**Shakuna
Jyotish**
Study of cosmic
omens, signs,
dreams, etc.

Darshan
(Philosophy)
Upanishads,
Puranas,
Sanghitas

**Ang Vidya
or Samudrik
Shastra**
Various body parts

Yoga

Metaphysics
Theosophy,
alchemy

**Modern
Sciences**
Ayurveda,
chemistry,
biology, physics,
geology,
medicine

**Hast
Jyotish**
Hands

**Paad
Jyotish**
Feet

**Mukha
Jyotish**
Face

**Vedic
Palmistry**

The dotted line in this chart traces the roots of
palmistry from the Vedic period to modern times.

The universe has organization and structure, from the largest galaxy to the tiniest atom.

THE VEDIC EXPLANATION FOR THE CREATION OF THE UNIVERSE

All attempts to explain the creation of the universe—whether scientific or metaphysical—involve a division of the One into the many. For example, most contemporary scientists explain the origin of the universe as an explosion of energy into matter—the big bang—which gave form to the known universe of galaxies, constellations, solar systems, and so on. In the Old Testament, God first creates heaven and earth, light and darkness, land and water, sun and moon, plants and animals, and finally, human beings, both male and female.

In virtually every belief system, whether scientific or religious, we see a pattern. There is a creative force (active, male, and positive), a receptive force (passive, female, and negative), and an energetic, dynamic force that vibrates between them, keeping them both united and separated.

The Vedic explanation for the creation of the universe states that before its existence, God—referred to as Purusha—existed as an unmanifested formless entity. The Book of John tells us: "In the beginning was the Word, and the Word was with God, and the Word was God." The Word is both separate from God (with God) and inseparable (was God).

The holy men of India perceived that the universe came into existence through the vibration of Aum, the "Word," and that the observable duality of positive and negative energies was held together in harmony by a third, neutral force.

We tend to think of duality as two separate and opposite extremes: light and dark, male and

The holy men of India perceived that the universe came into existence through the vibration of Aum, the "Word."

female, hot and cold. But how do we describe the point at which hot becomes cold, day becomes night, or active becomes passive? We tend to think of this neutral point as belonging to neither of the two extremes. For example, we think of dusk as the time between day and night, and we may think of this neutral time as being neither day nor night. Since it touches the two extremes, however, dusk contains elements of both day and night. Similarly, active and passive, positive and negative, have a neutral counterpart. This point is not-active/not-passive, not-positive/not-negative: it simply exists. What is neutral, then, is the force both binding the opposites and keeping them separate. This resonance between opposites is the life force of the universe. The concept of duality contains, therefore, an implied trinity.

THE THREE GUNAS: AN APPROACH TO THE THREE LEVELS OF AWARENESS

Since the essence of the Supreme Being is creative, God unfolded to become manifest in space and time. The formless Supreme Being (Parambrahma) created the universe. He drew upon the feminine aspect of himself—Mother Nature, or *prakriti*—to plant the seed of creation. In the process of calling manifest nature into being, Parambrahma, through the vibration of the divine word Aum, divided himself into three separate yet complementary aspects called *gunas*—*sattwa*, *rajas*, and *tamas*.

The three *gunas*, the building blocks of creation, are found woven throughout nature, and everything in the universe is influenced by the interplay of these three complementary threads. The *gunas* are represented in the Hindu trinity as Brahma the Creator, Vishnu the Preserver, and Shiva the Destroyer.

Sattwa or Brahma is the aspect of Parambrahma within us. It is that part of us called the soul. *Tamas* represents Shiva in the trinity and is the force of unbuilding, or destruction. It represents our physical nature, our body. *Rajas*, as the Vishnu aspect of the trinity, is the force of preservation. It relates to the mind. According to Vedic literature, Parambrahma (the One, God unmanifested) longed to share love. In order that we could partake in his love, he drew upon the force of Shiva (the Destroyer) to unbuild the structure of the One outward into the many—the manifested universe. From the original harmony of the trinity, Parambrahma unfolded into our human trinity of body, mind, and soul. In order for the many to realize the One, *rajas*, or Vishnu the Preserver, unites the desire or longing for love, *tamas*, or Shiva, with the object of love, *sattwa*, or Brahma. This balancing aspect of *rajas* is referred to as b*uddhi*—discriminating intelligence.

THE PRINCIPLE OF UNIVERSAL MAGNETISM

The metaphysical counterpart to the scientific theory of the big bang, in which the universe exploded from the cosmic egg, is that in the beginning, before any physical manifestation, there was an unmanifested yet omniscient creative intelligence whose thought gave birth to the physical three-dimensional reality of our universe. This creative energy, called the Prime Mover, or Parambrahma, became manifest in the physical universe as two opposing forces: attraction and repulsion, positive and negative, masculine and feminine.

Hindu metaphysics views the entire universe as one gigantic magnet, held together by two opposing forces. From the macro universe, to the solar system, to us as individuals, down to the smallest of subatomic particles, all things have the positive and negative polarity of a magnet. And like any magnet, our universe, and everything within it, has a central zone that is neither positive nor negative, but rather, like the original source point or center, is neutral. No matter how many times a magnet is split in half, it retains its opposite poles, and also its neutral center. Thus, at the heart of everything lies a neutral zone.

This dimensionless point plays a central role in evolution as the source from which the universe was created. If we see the purpose of life as the quest to free ourselves from duality to become one with the source of creation, then it would seem logical that the more we can access this central point by merging the opposing poles, the more we can regain our spiritual heritage (a reversal of the original "big bang").

The same electromagnetic dynamic found throughout the universe is also found in the hands. We are all human magnets: We attract or repel people and circumstances into and out of our lives. Each of us contains the aspects of both male and female, reason and feeling, body and soul. We can resolve our own duality by recognizing seeming opposites as aspects of a greater unity.

The three *gunas* demonstrate the principles of universal magnetism. The energy of *sattwa* is intrinsically positive and attracting. *Sattwa* seeks its origin, the formless spirit of God. The energy of *tamas* is intrinsically negative and repelling. The tendency of *tamas* is to separate from its origin. *Sattwa* and *tamas* are neither good nor bad but simply exhibit the qualities of the Supreme Spirit as manifested in the duality of existence. Ideally, the third aspect of this trinity, the neutral force *rajas*, balances these two extremes, harmoniously binding all three *gunas*.

The three *gunas*, working together, bind the imperishable soul to the body. When the mind knows that the body is the vehicle for the soul, the mind uses its discriminating intelligence to understand the truth of creation: that body, mind, and soul are one. As physical beings we understand our ultimate purpose at an intuitive or soul level; this purpose is to realize ourselves as spirit, belonging to the One. The dynamic resonance created as a result of this integration is equated to a physical state of ecstasy that in the East is referred to as *samadhi*, the union of body and soul.

When our minds become preoccupied with our physical nature, we begin to lose sight of our soul-self. We accept the illusion of ego, that we are separate beings with unique goals, desires, and abilities. The mind no longer functions simply as an intermediary between body and soul but starts to create its own "reality." The harmonious binding of the three *gunas* begins to unravel. Caught in the illusion of separateness, the mind seeks to express its dreams in the day-to-day world of the senses. The things of the world have importance for us: education, a good job, a comfortable home, congenial friends, and a fulfilling relationship. Our longing for love is turned outward toward the world rather than inward toward the soul. We may be aware of a body/mind duality but have forgotten that the mind's purpose is to integrate body, mind, and soul.

THE DYNAMIC OF AN INTEGRATED TRINITY: SATISFYING THE DESIRES OF THE HEART

The *gunas*, when integrated and working together, are experienced at every level as a perfect, balanced state of being wherein we feel unlimited peace and joy and attunement with our divine origin. The two opposing and destabilizing extremes of positive and negative, in a sense, become absorbed or "neutralized." On a physical level, this neutral feeling is experienced as a healthy body temperature of 37° Celsius—neither hot nor cold. This nonpolarity, when experienced on every level—body, mind, and soul—can be seen as a kind of reverse "big bang"

in which each of us, belonging to the many, ultimately becomes the One.

When the unmanifested (Parambrahma) divided into the manifested trinity of the three *gunas*, *sattwa* became the organs of the senses, the *jnanendriyas*: the nose, tongue, eyes, skin, and ears. These are concrete physical features. *Tamas* became the objects of the senses, the five *tanmatras*: the senses of smelling, tasting, seeing, touching, and hearing. These are abstract concepts that have their counterpart in the physical features. *Rajas* became the mechanisms of action, the *karmendriyas*: excretion, generation, motion (feet), manual skills (hands), and speech. These are activities or processes that allow us to realize the abstractions through what is concrete.

Harmony is established through the three *gunas* of *sattwa*, *rajas*, and *tamas* when, according to Swami Sri Yukteswar in *The Holy Science*, "the negative attributes of tamas—the five tanmatras—are united with the positive attributes of sattwa—the jnanendriyas—through the neutralizing power of the attributes of rajas—the karmendriyas, thereby satisfying the desires of the heart."*

THREE LEVELS OF CONSCIOUSNESS

The force of Mother Nature, or *prakriti*, is a complex one, consisting of many elements. From the

---

*Swami Sri Yukteswar, *The Holy Science* (Los Angeles: Self-Realization Fellowship, 1978), 9.

creative vibration of Aum resonate the *panchtattwas* (the five creative principles): *akasha* (ether), *vayu* (gas), *tejas* (fire), *appa* (liquids), and *kshiti* (solids).

All manifest creation, including mankind, exists first in the causal realm. This level of con-

sciousness is suffused by cosmic intelligence, or *chitta*. In the causal realm, there is an awareness of individuality but not separation from the Divine Self. Proceeding from creation is God's gift of free will. Discriminating intelligence (*buddhi*) allows us to realize that we are part of

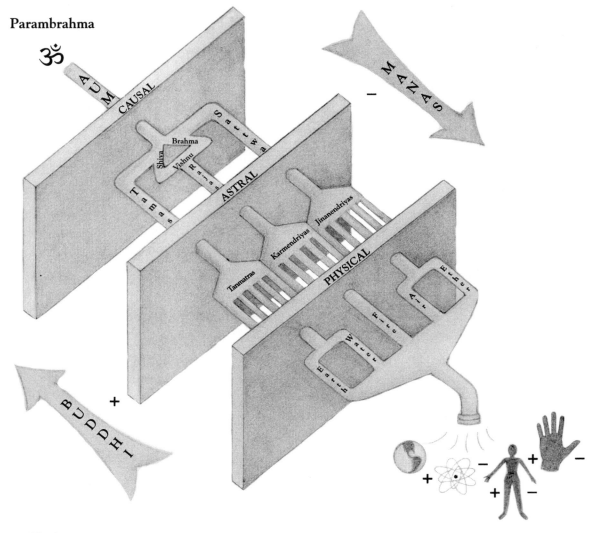

This diagram represents an Eastern perspective of the "big bang." Before creation Parambrahma, the one unmanifested force, manifested the three worlds—causal, astral, and physical—through the vibration of Aum. Manas, meaning "mind" in Sanskrit, is equated with the outward-going nature produced by the big bang. It is a force much like a ripple effect that leads us away from the unmanifest to the manifest. Buddhi (discriminating intelligence) reverses the process and reunites us with the unmanifest, a reverse big bang. By choosing to use our discriminating intelligence, we can, while in the physical body, realize the infinite within us.

the One. The ego, or *ahamkara*, the apparent center of personality, allows us to realize that we are individuals.

In the state of *ahamkara*, or ego, we have choices. We may use our awareness of individuality to remain centered in the Divine Self. Here, we are exercising *buddhi*. Conversely, we may think of ourselves as independent, self-sufficient beings apart from the One. Here, the mind, or *manas* (sense consciousness) accepts the illusion of otherness. The process of unfolding away from the center now takes us to the astral realm, the second level of consciousness.

The mind requires senses through which to experience its individuality—the organs of longing (*tanmatras*), which are smelling, tasting, seeing, touching, and hearing. These are abstract concepts that have their counterpart in the physical features (the nose, tongue, eyes, skin, and ears). The mind also requires the motor organs—the five instruments of action (*karmendriyas*), which are excretion, reproduction, walking, handling, and speech. These are activities or processes that allow us to realize abstractions through the concrete. The mind further requires the organs of cognition (*jnanendriyas*)—the nose, tongue, eyes, skin, and ears. These are concrete physical features.

The four powers of the causal realm—*chitta*, *buddhi*, *ahamkara*, and *manas*—and the fifteen powers in the astral level give rise to the powers of the physical realm—the *mahabhutas* (gross elements): ether, air, fire, water, and earth.

The three levels of consciousness—causal,

The three levels of consciousness—causal, astral, and physical— are exemplified in the process by which Alexander Graham Bell realized his invention of the telephone.

astral, and physical—are evidenced, for example, in the process by which Alexander Graham Bell realized his invention of the telephone. First came the idea (the causal level) of being able to speak with another person at a distance. Next came the unfolding of the concept into research, scientific equations, and diagrams (the astral level), the blueprints of the invention. Last came the actual product, which involved physical materials such as electrical components (the physical level).

THE CONCEPT OF MAYA

In day-to-day living, most of us are more aware of the physical dimension than of the astral or causal levels. We see ourselves as unique, independent beings separate from each other and, except in some philosophical, abstract way, apart from God. According to Vedic teaching, this is the illusion of human existence known as *maya*. The more we search for joy, for awareness, for reality outside of ourselves, the more it will elude us, for true joy, true awareness, and true reality exist in the infinite, the Divine Self, of which we are a part.

In day-to-day living, most of us are more aware of the physical dimension than of the astral or causal levels.

Graphically, the Sanskrit character Aum symbolizes the interplay of energy of the three gunas.

THE SYMBOL OF AUM

One of the difficulties of attempting to describe the process through which God created the universe is that we are limited by finite human terminology. Perhaps the closest we can come to an explanation for the creation of the universe is through analogy. Therefore, the Vedas used the symbol of Aum to represent the process of creation.

In writing down their understanding of Aum, the universal "song" of creation, the Hindu sages constructed a symbol that characterizes both the unity and diversity of creation and the relationship that exists between Creator and creation. The Aum symbol is seen as a microcosm of the universe or macrocosm.

Graphically, the Sanskrit character Aum symbolizes the interplay of energy of the three *gunas*. At the top rests a horizontal arc with a dot at its center. This stands for Parambrahma or God, the unmanifested original creative source, the "One." Below this arc lies the main body of the symbol, which suggests that the "One has become the many"—the physical, manifested universe. At the center lies the seed of the Aum symbol. Three separate lines extend from this point, representing threads of energy or consciousness—the *gunas*. The upper line extends in a counterclockwise direction, representing *sattwa*. The lower line extends in a clockwise direction, representing *tamas*. The third line extends horizontally from the point where the other two lines meet, representing *rajas*. The shape of this line mirrors the upper horizontal arc, Parambrahma.

MANAS: THE DIVIDED SELF

What we have been describing up until now is the state of harmony represented by the interrelationship of the three *gunas* in the Aum symbol. This is the ideal to which every human being aspires. It is achieved when the discriminating intelligence (*buddhi*) guides our *tamasic* desires toward an awareness of an attunement with our soul-self, *sattwa*.

Throughout life, we are presented with choices. The decisions we make may either promote a state of harmony in our being or divide us from our true nature. The success of the outcome of these choices depends on how appropriately we are able to draw upon our *rajasic* force. When we allow our *tamasic* longings to be guided by *buddhi*, we are appropriately using our *rajas* force. For example, the sensation of taste *(tamas)* is actualized through the taste buds *(sattwa)*. But if our longing to taste is not tempered by *buddhi*, this desire can lead to abuses such as eating disorders or food addictions.

It is a temptation to become preoccupied with the immediate gratification of our longings and desires, our *tamas* nature. We may see this gratification as an end in itself. When we learn, however, to use our sensory intelligence in a discriminating fashion, we realize that our ultimate desire is to be united with our soul-self. We intuitively recognize that the longing nature of *tamas*, properly channeled, can lead us toward an increasing awareness of spirit *(sattwa)* and, hence, a greater self-understanding.

When our *rajas* force is directed through appropriate choices under the guidance of *buddhi*, we find ourselves in a state of balance. Conversely, we find ourselves in a state of imbalance, literally separated from our soul-self, when our *rajas* force is misdirected through inappropriate choices *(manas)*. If we do not exercise *buddhi* when faced with making a decision, our personal biases, fears, or misconceptions may cause us to form opinions and draw conclusions based on personal, subjective reasoning. In

Throughout life, we are presented with choices. The decisions we make may either promote a state of harmony in our being or divide us from our true nature.

buddhi our mind acts as a vehicle through which the intuition relays information. It is intuition—our inner wisdom—that provides us with unfailing guidance in making choices.

THE JOURNEY HOME

We all have an instinctive longing to be connected to someone or something beyond ourselves. We reach out to our family, our friends, our community, our careers, and our culture to help us define who we are. When we lose a loved one, when we move away from our friends, or when we start a new career, our sense of loss may cause us to feel that we have left a part of ourselves behind. Our solitude, however, offers us an opportunity to realize the essence of our true nature. Rather than looking to others to satisfy our instinctive longing for connectedness, we are forced to look within ourselves.

This sense of "self" as separate from "other" is part of our understanding of the inherent duality of the universe. As we have seen in our discussion of the *gunas*, however, duality is, in fact, an illusion. There is a point at which self becomes other, and the other is self. This center point is the place of greatest stillness and greatest power. By finding the center within us, we realize that we can never be separated from those we love, nor do we need to identify ourselves as being only a part of something. We are those we love and they are us, we can reach the Supreme Being within ourselves, and the many become the One.

In today's world, our preoccupation with being independent and asserting our individuality has led to an ever increasing sense of alienation. Our social and political structures are becoming more decentralized. Economic boom-and-depression cycles and worldwide struggles to assert national or religious identity are creating global geographical redefinition. New technologies, designed to make our lives easier, provide less direct human contact. Most people change careers three to six times in their lives. Even the idioms of the language we speak betray our sense of alienation. In moments of crises, we speak of being "beside ourselves." We feel lost, cut off not only from others, but from our true nature. We may take some time off to "find ourselves." But where do we look? Many of us turn to travel or new friends; we may acquire a new hobby or interest, find a new partner, or go into therapy. We look outside ourselves to cure a problem that we recognize intuitively as an inner malaise.

Why do these methods not work for us? Or, if they do seem to work for a while, why do they not effect lifelong changes? Although in our hearts and souls we may experience a longing for reunion with something or someone or a force we cannot explain, our minds have accepted the illusion that we are unique, separate beings. If we have a religious belief, we may think of God as a somewhat remote and awesome Being—certainly beyond and outside our mortal selves. Many established faiths hold to the concept of a life after earthly existence, which is the reward for living a good life, and in which we stand face-to-face with our

Creator. Yet Vedic teaching tells us that we do not have to wait until we die to experience the bliss of God; we can realize the world of the spirit or soul in this life.

VEDIC PALMISTRY: FINDING AUM IN THE HAND

Over the centuries, many techniques have been devised to help us find harmony. Palmistry was developed as a method through which the degree of integration among the forces of *sattwa*, *rajas*, and *tamas* within the individual could be determined by examining the markings on the hand.

As we have seen, according to Eastern thought, the physical body that we can see and touch is considered to be only one of three bodies. It is interpenetrated by a second, the astral body, which has a higher and finer rate of vibration; the astral body is the refined energy template that gives rise to the physical body, which is structured and maintained according to the specifications of the astral body. The third body, known as the causal body, has an even subtler rate of vibration than the other two. It forms the true basis of the person's being, the original "idea" for which the person was created.

In the study of *hast jyotish*, when we look into the lines and signs of the hand, we are really looking at the reflection of the astral and causal bodies in the physical body. *Rajas*, the mind (the astral level), as an interface between *sattwa*, the soul (the causal level), and *tamas*, the body (the physical level), has the ability through *buddhi* to unify the three *gunas*. When the body, mind, and soul are integrated, we become whole, or complete, and feel harmonious. Since each of us carries in our palm a personalized signature that represents the sum total of our experiences, attitudes, memories, and thoughts, a study of our handprints can reveal the degree of harmony (achieved through *buddhi*) or imbalance (resulting from *manas*) in our lives.

In the next chapter, we will examine specific features in the hand with regard to their degree of balance, and look at how to restore equilibrium when it is missing. We will begin with a step-by-step look at all the factors that comprise the geography of the hand.

2

The Geography of the Hand

THE THREE LEVELS OF AWARENESS
IN THE HAND

We live in an electromagnetic universe, with the atom constituting its basic building block. As physical beings, we know that, in common with everything in the universe, we too are made up of atoms. Atoms in general are characterized by stability; they are electrically neutral because every atom contains the same number of protons (positive charge) as electrons (negative charge). We can observe the balance inherent in the patterns of creation with a scanning electron microscope, a high-powered telescope, or even the naked eye.

Fundamental to all living entities is the principle of balance. For example, a chemical imbalance may result in deformity or disease. With sufficient scientific knowledge, we can restore the organism to a balanced condition.

As human beings, we are more than the sum of our physical parts. In addition to our bodies, we possess minds and spirits. We are able to observe our mind nature by being conscious of ourselves as thinking beings, and we are able to observe our spiritual nature by intuition. We have a tendency, however, to give certain components of our nature precedence over others. For example, you may vote for a politician on the basis of her media persona rather than the intellectual or ethical content of her campaign platform. The absentminded scholar may become so absorbed in his theories that he forgets to go to the dentist and may wear the same

23

Everywhere in nature, from the macro universe, to the solar system, to each of us as individuals, right down to a single atom, we find the attributes of the three gunas—sattwa, rajas, and tamas—the trinity of causal, astral, and physical—soul, mind, body—light, energy, matter—and the magnetic properties of positive, neutral, and negative.

socks for a week. A person embarking on a spiritual journey may tend to forgo empathy for others whom he judges to be less enlightened. This shortsightedness can lead to misunderstanding in relationships.

Once we recognize that the ideal human being is a balanced construct of body, mind, and spirit, we have taken the first step toward self-realization. Our attunement to the degree of harmony in our nature allows us to make conscious choices about the direction of our lives. Since it is our true nature to be balanced, we can exercise our free will to help restore harmony in our being.

Three Levels of Consciousness

Most of us are familiar with the psychological terms *conscious* and *subconscious* in reference to the duality of body/mind. By extension, then, we can accept the term *superconscious* to refer to the soul level of consciousness. In Hindu writings, the conscious, subconscious, and superconscious levels are referred to as physical, astral, and causal. The three levels of consciousness also correspond to the three *gunas*: The causal level is *sattwic*; the astral level is *rajasic*; and the physical level is *tamasic*. The degree of balance or harmony at all levels of consciousness depends on the balance of the *gunas* throughout our entire conscious, subconscious, and superconscious being.

According to Vedic literature, we are made up of three bodies, the causal, astral, and physical, which correspond to sattwa, rajas, *and* tamas.

The Three Gunas

In Hindu sacred writings, the balance of soul, mind, and body is explained by the concept of the three *gunas*. The *gunas* operate at all levels of palmistry and are the basis for all structures in the hand, both large and small.

In order to illustrate the function of the *gunas* in palmistry, let's use the analogy of holography. In a hologram, a three-dimensional image is produced with lasers. If the hologram is broken in half, its two smaller pieces will retain the identical image of the original. No matter how many times the fragments are split, the results will be the same—ever smaller yet completely identical images.

Continuing with the hologram analogy, let's imagine that the "macro" image is itself a fragment of a much larger hologram. The new macro image is, of course, identical except in scale. The "macro" hand has a similar relationship to the entire body, which displays the dynamic of the three *gunas*. We can continue to play with the idea of macro/micro to explain the interrelationship of all living things in the universe. The concept of macro/micro, then, depends on our point of reference, which, in palmistry, is the hands.

THE STRUCTURE OF THE HAND

In palmistry, we can see the dynamic of the *gunas* balancing soul, mind, and body (*sattwa*, *rajas*, and *tamas*) in the hand itself. The mind (*rajas*) is responsible for directing the body (*tamas*) to be used for the noble, ideal purposes for which

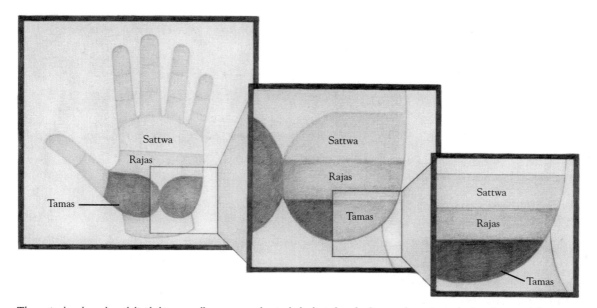

The entire hand can be subdivided into smaller segments that include the palm, the fingers, the major and minor lines, and the mounts. From macro (the entire hand) to micro (each specific feature of the hand), we can see the dynamic of sattwa, rajas, *and* tamas *at play.*

it was intended—as a vehicle through which we can fulfill our life's karmic obligations. We can choose to follow the route of the soul (*sattwa*) or we can choose to satisfy immediate sensory desires (*tamas*). Choices based on *buddhi* (discriminating intelligence) help us progress in our evolution, whereas choices based on *manas* (delusion) impede our growth.

Most of us make a distinction between our public and private lives. The choices we make regarding our behavior when we are at our job are usually dictated by the conventions of the workplace. For example, a junior worker knows not to yell at his boss regardless of the provocation. This does not necessarily mean that his choice to be deferential is based on bud*dhi*. The same person may give in to his *manas* nature by spreading rumors about his boss over drinks with his buddies. A generous and courtly manner in the workplace may or may not reflect a harmonious disposition. On the other hand, an open, loving attitude toward our immediate family may be more indicative of our true nature.

Specific areas of the hand will reveal details describing our deeply ingrained character traits. Within them, we can see how our thoughts over many lifetimes have resulted in our present attitudes and circumstances. Greater balance within these micro areas of the hand shows that we are developing a presence of mind, a serenity that enables us to control our instinctive nature. We become aware of the universal nature of spirit, and, as a result, we recognize the needs of others.

The entire hand can be subdivided into smaller segments that include the palm, the fingers, the major and minor lines, and the mounts. From macro (the entire hand) to micro (each specific feature of the hand), we can see the dynamic of *sattwa*, *rajas*, and *tamas* at play. The *gunas*, therefore, can help us determine the degree of balance we are experiencing in our life, both generally and specifically.

The study of the entire hand reveals the nature of our public persona. The palm shows how we would like to behave—our inner resolve. The fingers show how able we are to transform our intentions into actual behavior.

When the *gunas* are balanced throughout the hand, our social selves, our intentions, and our expression of those intentions are integrated. What we mean is what we do, and what we show to the public is an accurate representation of who we really are.

THE HAND: A REFLECTION OF OUR PUBLIC SELF

According to *hast jyotish*, the balance of the three *gunas* in the hand reflects how we present ourselves to the outside world. Most of us have acquired the basic social skills that enable us to function in a civilized manner. Normally, our interaction with the public does not make demands that greatly affect our personal freedom or comfort. For example, we may let someone go ahead of us in the checkout aisle at the grocery store if they have only one item to pur-

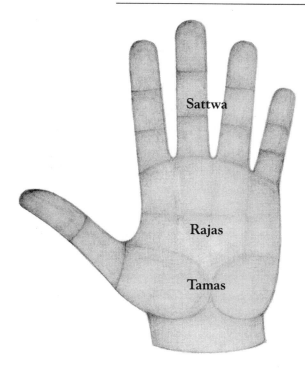

According to hast jyotish, *the balance of the three* gunas *in the hand reflects how we present ourselves to the outside world.*

and the base of the palm correspond to *sattwa, rajas,* and *tamas,* respectively.

THE PALM:
BEHIND THE SCENE

The palm indicates ingrained patterns of thinking that have shaped our attitudes and behavior over many lifetimes. From birth we are taught how to interact with those around us. Ideally, we become socialized, behaving in accordance with the customs and traditions of our culture. As a consequence of our social training, however, we may disguise a deeper, fundamental way of thinking and behaving that is purely instinctive and spontaneous. These uninhibited, knee-jerk reactions to circumstance are the best indicators of how fully we have embraced the behavior we exhibit socially. This primal aspect of our nature is indicated in our palm.

The degree of integration of the *gunas* in the palm indicates the degree of control that we have over our instinctive nature. For example, we may run out into a busy intersection to rescue a child who is about to be hit by a car. In that instant, we override our instinct for survival by disregarding our personal safety. We recognize the essential unity of all souls when our instinctive behavior extends to embrace others. The mental realm of *rajas,* shown by our recognition of the child's need, the spiritual realm of *sattwa,* shown by our intuitive understanding that we are one with the child, and the physical realm of *tamas,* shown by our instinctive reaching out to

chase and we have many. In this case, the benefits of our action outweigh the inconvenience. If we discover, however, that this person has lost her keys and wallet, would we offer to pay for her groceries and drive her home? If we have just won the lottery, we might find it easy to perform an altruistic act; but our worry about having to pay our own bills may cause us to hesitate. In choosing to be generous we are exercising our buddhi nature; in choosing to be self-protective we are satisfying our *manas* or ego.

The fingers, the upper section of the palm,

save the child, operate in harmony. The *gunas* become integrated as we learn to transcend the personal in favor of the impersonal. We dissolve the dualistic illusion that separates self or ego from the whole of humanity. This potential is seen in the interaction among the body, mind, and soul divisions of the palm.

Palmistry recognizes a threefold division within the palm that represents the three levels of consciousness. The mounts of Jupiter, Saturn, Sun, and Mercury in the upper third outline the *sattwic* world of the palm. The mounts of Mars negative and Mars positive, which border the mount of Rahu at the center of the palm,

are *rajasic* in nature. The lower third is defined by the mounts of Venus, Luna, and Ketu, which are *tamasic*. These mounts are usually more pronounced than those of the other two worlds.

THE FINGERS: LINKING US TO THE WORLD

In the fingers, *sattwa*, *rajas*, and *tamas* are reflected in the top, middle, and base phalanxes. The fingers act as a channel through which we consciously express who we are. The mounts, with their overlay of lines and signs, indicate

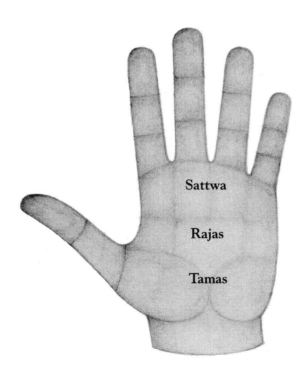

The degree of integration of the gunas in the palm indicates the degree of control that we have over our instinctive nature.

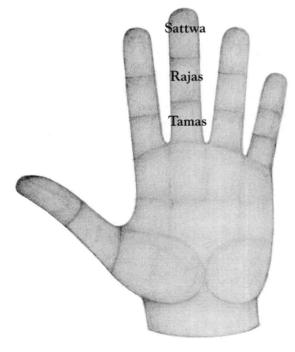

The balance in the three phalanxes of sattwa, rajas, *and* tamas *reveals the extent to which we can achieve the potential shown on the palm.*

our thoughts, ideas, and feelings. The formation and placement of the fingers, including the phalanxes, show how freely we are able to express our thoughts and feelings beyond ourselves into the outside world.

Balance among the three phalanxes indicates that the mind (*rajas*) is integrated with spirit (*sattwa*) and body (*tamas*). Their harmonious interrelation shows that whatever we communicate to others is an accurate representation of our true nature.

Imbalance among the phalanxes shows that our conscious expression, the fingers—like the visible part of an iceberg—does not conform to our superconscious, the mounts—the unseen portion of the iceberg that lies below the surface. For example, a new acquaintance who appears to be friendly and outgoing may prove in time to harbor an angry and vindictive nature. In many instances, behavior indicated by a disparity between the mounts and fingers reveals itself under trying circumstances, when our "true colors" surface.

The Phalanxes

The fingers reflect the conscious self. The palm contains the mounts, which relate to our deeply held superconscious beliefs, whereas the fingers reflect the conscious way we deal with the stored energy of the mounts. By studying the length and shape of the three phalanxes of the fingers, we can track how well we are making use of our potential for self-expression. The fingers carry many nerve endings that give information about the organic strength of the brain. Therefore,

they are able to reveal the extent to which we can achieve the potential shown on the palm.

Each finger is divided into three phalanxes. Each of these phalanxes relates to one of three worlds, *sattwa*, *rajas*, and *tamas*. The degree to which these worlds are balanced in relation to one another can be seen in various characteristics such as the shape of a phalanx, its width and length, what markings are present, and so forth.

The phalanx closest to the palm, which is *tamasic*, reflects the degree to which our body provides a supportive foundation for our initiatives. It relates to our survival instincts: eating, sleeping, mating, and so on.

The middle phalanx, which is *rajasic*, shows our awareness of our environment and the degree of our attunement to others.

The top phalanx, which is *sattwic*, reflects qualities of discipline, foresight, and the degree

Balanced phalanxes.

of our understanding of how to direct our physical energy productively in the world around us.

Balanced Phalanxes

Ideally, the three phalanxes should be equal in length. When balanced, the bottom phalanx reflects an ability to nurture our body without being identified with physical needs and cravings; the top phalanx indicates an ability to direct our energies positively; the middle phalanx shows that we have a good sense of our social interaction and our particular role in the world.

If we lack the equanimity to balance all three phalanxes, we decrease our potential to exhibit the positive qualities attributed to the finger wherein the phalanx is located.

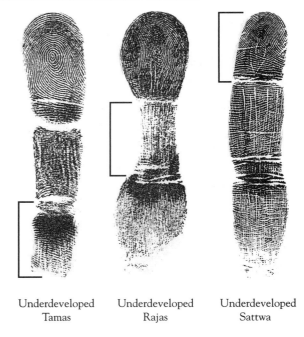

Underdeveloped   Underdeveloped   Underdeveloped
Tamas   Rajas   Sattwa

Underdeveloped phalanxes.

Overdeveloped   Overdeveloped   Overdeveloped
Tamas   Rajas   Sattwa

Overdeveloped phalanxes.

Overdeveloped Phalanxes

An overdeveloped bottom phalanx shows a preoccupation with our physical needs at the expense of our own productivity and ability to serve others. An overdeveloped middle phalanx suggests a strong awareness of others and can sometimes be considered a sign of wisdom. It denotes humanitarian and philanthropic qualities. An overdeveloped top phalanx indicates a tendency to be too opinionated and egotistical.

Underdeveloped Phalanxes

An underdeveloped bottom phalanx shows a tendency to neglect our physical needs. We need to look after ourselves in order to support our resolution to be productive. An underdeveloped middle phalanx suggests a lack of attunement to the needs of those around us. Since there is a higher concentration of nerve endings in the fingertips, an underdeveloped top phalanx suggests that we are prone to defensive behavior. An underdeveloped top phalanx also indicates a lack of foresight, endurance, and discipline. We need to develop nervous stamina, which will allow us to become more tolerant and patient.

Correspondences Between the Phalanxes and the Signs of the Zodiac

If we exclude the thumb, with its phalanx of will (top portion) and its phalanx of logic (lower portion) we see that the remaining four fingers

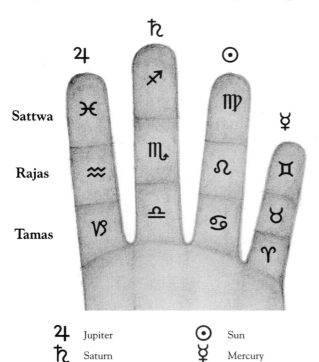

Jupiter	Sun
Saturn	Mercury

Index finger (Jupiter), middle finger (Saturn), ring finger (Sun), and the small finger (Mercury).

are made up of a total of twelve phalanxes, each of which corresponds to a different sign of the zodiac. Aries, Taurus, and Gemini are found consecutively on the *tamas*, *rajas*, and *sattwa* worlds of the Mercury finger. The sequence continues with Cancer, Leo, and Virgo beginning with the physical phalanx of the Sun finger. On Saturn we find Libra, Scorpio, and Sagittarius, and on the finger of Jupiter, we can locate Capricorn, Aquarius, and Pisces.

THE MOUNTS AND MAJOR AND MINOR LINES

The interplay of the three levels of awareness can be seen through the interrelationship of the mounts, the major lines, and the minor lines. In this dynamic, the mounts represent *sattwa*, the soul or superconscious, which is the foundation of our being. The minor lines represent *tamas*, the ego or conscious mind. The subconscious, or *rajas*, is represented by the major lines and enables us to understand the language of the superconscious (soul). It is important to consider each of these aspects of the palm in relation to the other two, not as isolated phenomena.

The *sattwic*, the intuitive or soul level, is not perceivable in isolation from the major and minor lines. The *rajasic*, or subconscious major lines—much like an interpreter who facilitates conversation for those who speak a different language—allow us to perceive the superconscious at a conscious level. Minor lines, then, appear as a result of our growing recognition that there is a greater reality beyond that which we experience on an instinctive, sensate level. The *sattwic* intuitive wisdom of the soul is made manifest at a conscious, *tamasic* level through the agency of *rajas*, the translator.

As we progress in our evolution toward self-awareness, we learn to listen to our soul voice. This progress is demonstrated by the refinement in the shape and quality of the mounts, the major lines, and the minor lines. The development of this intuitive sixth sense indicates that we are learning to integrate *sattwa*, *rajas*, and *tamas* on all levels of awareness—conscious, subconscious, and superconscious.

The Mounts

The mounts are the fleshy pads found on the palm. They represent the ground or foundation upon which the major and minor lines record the progress of our individual soul consciousness *(ahamkara)* in this incarnation. The Divine Light—God—is made manifest in the mounts of the hand, just as pure light manifests in the colors of a rainbow. In Vedic teaching, each of the mounts is associated with a corresponding color, with the entire palm representing the full color spectrum. Ideally, when we are able to integrate all areas of our lives in perfect harmony, we reflect the Divine Light.

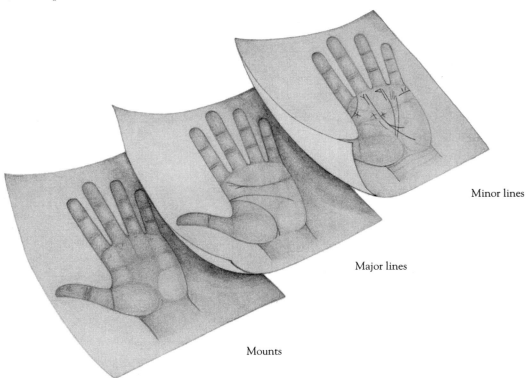

Minor lines

Major lines

Mounts

The interplay of the three levels of awareness can be seen through the interrelationship of the mounts, the major lines, and the minor lines.

By cultivating an attunement to our superconscious—our link to the infinite—we can become free within ourselves. We recognize the unlimited possibilities of soul, unfettered by the restrictions of mind. We need to develop this spiritual side of our nature, however, through choices that are based on *buddhi*. Otherwise, the mounts may reflect a personalized, subjective (*manas*) view of the universe with ourselves or ego at its center, rather than reflecting a growing awareness of soul.

Balance found within each mount, and among the mounts as a whole, reflects a grow-ing awareness of our universal soul nature. In the following evolutionary sequence, the ideal expression of each mount is described.

The Evolutionary Sequence of the Mounts

According to Vedic teaching, when the One be-comes the many, each soul embarks on a journey of many lifetimes. Just as the Divine Self longed to share love, so each of us longs to be reunited with the One. Each successive lifetime provides us with the opportunity to evolve to the point

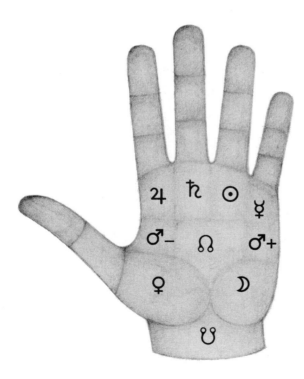

The mounts are the fleshy pads found on the palm.
Each is associated with a planet
or a node of the moon.

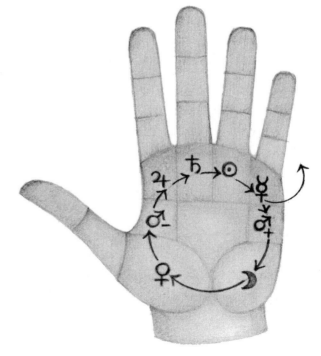

There are seven mounts, and each of their
planetary associations represents a distinct function or
aspect of the evolutionary cycle of life.

where our awareness of ourselves as individuals does not separate us from one another or from the Creator. Once we attain this soul self-awareness, we have no further need for successive cycles of incarnation.

There are seven mounts, each of which is associated with a specific astrological planet (or node of the moon) that represents a distinct function or aspect of the evolutionary cycle of life. The mounts depict both a sequence of spiritual growth and a unified process of development in which no one step is more important than any other. The mounts might be compared to a combination lock consisting of a series of numbers that must be entered in a particular sequence to enable the lock to function.

The mount of Luna relates to the idea or concept of existence. It represents the blueprint of our life shaped by previous incarnations as well as lessons learned from astral teachers. The mount of Venus is associated with the actual formation or conception of the physical body. The mounts of Luna and Venus are located in the *tamasic* realm of the hand.

The mount of Mars—actually two mounts known as the Mars galaxy—reflects our autonomous existence from the moment we take our first breath, seen in Mars negative, until we relinquish our last breath at the moment of death, seen in Mars positive. The Mars galaxy is located in the *rajasic* realm of the hand.

The next four mounts—Jupiter, Saturn, Sun, and Mercury—are located in the *sattwic* realm of the hand. The mount of Jupiter indicates the degree of our self-awareness and the level of knowledge we have about the purpose and direction of our life. The mount of Saturn shows the extent to which we become wise through experience and self-examination. The energy of Saturn reveals the discipline we need in order to fulfill our destiny. The mount of the Sun indicates the degree to which we are motivated to share our wisdom and knowledge. Our interaction with others can attract public attention and worldly success; the mount of Mercury reveals our freedom from attachment to our success or reputation. Mercury represents our potential for complete liberation.

The most spiritually advanced saints and yogis realize that they are one with all things, that their bodies are merely physical manifestations of spirit. They may not even think of death as the letting go of the last breath, heartbeat, and thought. Death becomes total freedom. When their bodies die, all bonds to the physical dissolve and they reunite with the Divine. They may have no need to be reborn. In the evolutionary cycle of the mounts, the spiritually advanced soul realizes itself to be in the causal realm, registering this perception in the mount of Mercury. It does not experience the moment of death as a separation, but simply as a metamorphosis from body/mind/spirit to pure spirit.

Most of us, however, have only glimpses of the saints' realization that we are one with all things. We see ourselves as separate beings because we perceive our physical body more immediately than our spirit. With our last breath, thought, and heartbeat, registered in Mars positive, we perceive death as a loss. Our consciousness is still tied to physical existence and, therefore, has longings that seek to be fulfilled through successive karmic cycles. We need to be reborn. And so our soul consciousness remains in the astral realm until it is prepared to adopt physical form once again.

Let us examine the characteristics of each mount in terms of its balanced, underdeveloped, and overdeveloped characteristics.

Luna

The Sanskrit word for Luna, or the Moon, is Chandra. The mount of Luna represents the birth of creation—the force of Shakti or Mother Nature. Luna relates to the mind or internal organs of perception and cognition, the instruments by which the five senses of tasting, touching, seeing, hearing, and smelling affect the soul. This awareness of the self perceiving itself through the senses gives rise to an aware-ness of the self as a separate being. Luna represents the mind of Shakti.

The formation of this mount reflects how we filter the constant flood of information that is being channeled and received through the senses. Luna indicates to what degree our thoughts, feelings, and perception of reality are objective, lucid, and clear or subjective, confused, and hallucinatory. An ideal Luna shows that we can be creative, imaginative, and inspired, that we use our senses to uplift and nurture others. An underdeveloped Luna indicates either that we lack imagination or that we suffer from imagined fears, insecurity, and oversensitivity. Our ability to perceive the joy of creation is overshadowed by negativity. We can learn to become more positive in our outlook by appreciating the beauty in each moment.

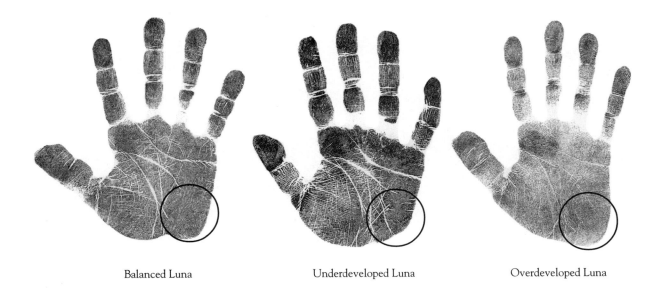

Balanced Luna   Underdeveloped Luna   Overdeveloped Luna

The three levels of development of Luna.

An overdeveloped Luna is an indication of a craving for constant sensual gratification. We may not be sensitive to the needs of others because we are preoccupied with our own quest for excitement. We should make a conscious effort to balance our need for stimulation with an appropriate regard for the happiness of others.

Venus

The Sanskrit word for Venus is Shukra, which means "bright," "radiant," the "essence of things." Venus represents the physical body that houses the senses. The nose, tongue, skin, eyes, and ears are the physical counterparts to the senses indicated by the mount of Luna. Our sex drive, procreative fluids, and outward appearance are also physical aspects relating to Venus. This mount indicates whether we are appropriately using the body—our physical vehicle—to evolve and fulfill our karmic obligations in life. Venus is also an indicator of our potential to love unconditionally, which is the ideal expression and utility of our body and senses. Venus represents the body of Shakti.

An underdeveloped Venus indicates a lack of enthusiasm or vitality for life. We may feel listless and indifferent. We need to take care of our physical bodies, through proper diet, sleep, and exercise, so that we can participate in the joy of living. An overdeveloped Venus reflects an obsession with physical pleasure. We have too great an attachment to beautiful clothes, gourmet food, fine material possessions, and sexual gratification. We need to channel our delight in physical pleasure into an opportunity to give comfort to others.

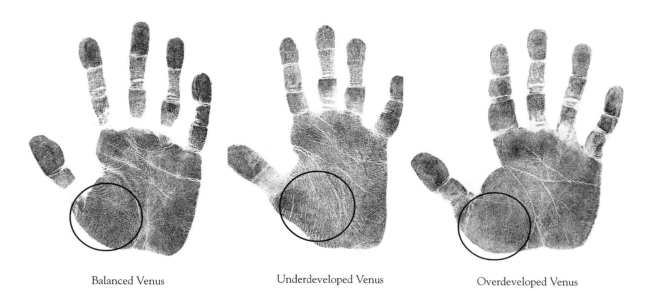

Balanced Venus   Underdeveloped Venus   Overdeveloped Venus

The three levels of development of Venus.

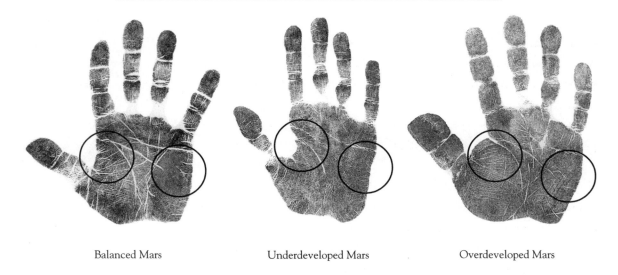

Balanced Mars   Underdeveloped Mars   Overdeveloped Mars

The three levels of development of Mars.

Mars

There are two mounts of Mars in the hand, Mars negative and Mars positive, which together are known as the Mars galaxy. This galaxy is referred to as the Kalpnic path or path of existence. The Sanskrit word for Mars is Mangal, which translates as "auspicious beginning." It represents our first breath or instinct for survival. The Mars galaxy indicates the degree of assertiveness or passivity with which we embrace life from our first breath in Mars negative to our last breath in Mars positive.

The terms *positive* and *negative* are used here in the context of polarity and not in a judgmental sense, that is, as meaning good or bad. Mars positive is found on the percussion (the edge of the palm below the fourth finger) of the hand. It relates to our mental strength. Ideally, Mars

positive indicates an ability to choose not to react instinctively but to be calm and controlled under all circumstances. Mars negative is located on the thumb side of the hand. It relates to our emotional and physical strength, our instinct for survival. It indicates the potential of our nervous system to withstand the shocks that come to us in life. Ideally, the energy of Mars negative supports the good intentions that are conceptualized in Mars positive. The Mars galaxy represents the warrior force within us, our determination to embrace the challenges of life while respecting the rights of others.

An underdeveloped Mars galaxy suggests that we accept defeat too readily and that we do not have the stamina to overcome obstacles. By setting attainable goals for ourselves and achieving them, we can build up our energy. In

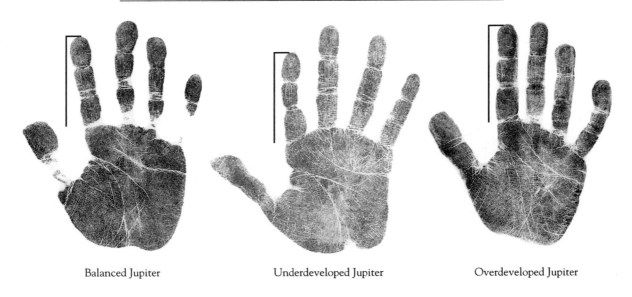

Balanced Jupiter   Underdeveloped Jupiter   Overdeveloped Jupiter

The three levels of development of Jupiter.

this way, we develop confidence, endurance, and hence, initiative. An overdeveloped Mars galaxy indicates that we have such a strong sense of our own existence that we may assert ourselves at the expense of others. We need to temper our overabundant energy so as not to crush the initiative of others. Mars also relates to the life force—the energy within all matter. Energy is analogous to fire; used with discrimination it sustains life; out of control, it can destroy.

Jupiter

Brahaspati, the Sanskrit name for Jupiter, literally translates as "the guru of all the gods." The word *guru* itself means "dispeller of darkness." As the first mount in the *sattwic* realm, Jupiter reflects our awareness that we are part of a greater whole, that we have a purpose in life beyond survival. While we have a unique role to play in society, our purpose is to complement, not to be in competition with, each other, and thus the illusion that we are separate from one another is dispelled. Ideally, Jupiter indicates that we have the desire to find our purpose in life. It shows the extent of our efforts made to accomplish our goals while maintaining respect for the needs and aspirations of others. An underdeveloped Jupiter reveals a lack of purpose. This may lead to an inferiority complex or a sense of futility. We need to ask ourselves what our goals are or seek the company of others who can help us discover our purpose. An overdeveloped Jupiter shows an overidentification with the role we play in society. We are susceptible to vanity, self-importance, and arrogance. We may have a desire to dominate, which causes us to become more and more isolated. Once we understand that we are at the mercy of others' recognition,

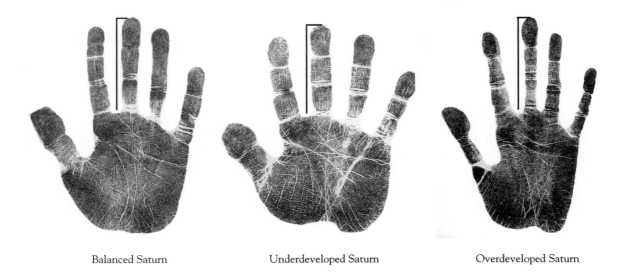

| Balanced Saturn | Underdeveloped Saturn | Overdeveloped Saturn |

The three levels of development of Saturn.

we become free to develop self-reliance and respect for both ourselves and others.

Saturn

The Saturn mount and finger lie in the vertical center of the hand in the *sattwic* realm. The Sanskrit word for Saturn is Shani, from *shan*, which translates as "quiet," "soft," or "calm." Saturn is sometimes referred to as the mount of "blessings in disguise." It gives rise to the longest finger, which is often seen as a barometer of difficult circumstances in our lives. These difficulties cause us to become introspective. We delve into the depths of our nature to find answers, interior strength, and hence, wisdom.

Saturn represents the spine, an indicator of our inner strength and integrity. The mount and finger of Saturn show to what extent we are able to make wise decisions based on our ability to integrate reason and feeling. Saturn makes good mediators and judges. Saturn is the philosopher. It shows our potential for being objective and honest in all circumstances and for perceiving the truth without prejudice. Saturn also shows our ability to structure our lives and to be disciplined in achieving our goals.

An underdeveloped Saturn indicates an inability to show proper judgment. In this case we have a tendency not to be aware of the long-term consequences of our words and actions. We need to curb our predisposition to impetuosity, which may lead to thoughtless behavior. An overdeveloped Saturn shows too much restraint, leading to coldness, pessimism, and a lack of spontaneity. In this case we need to disentangle ourselves from too much thinking and balance the coolness of introspection with the warmth of empathy.

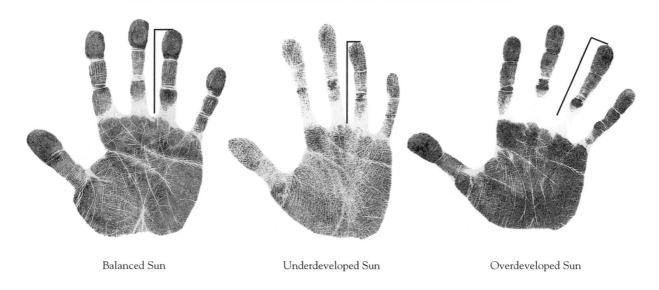

Balanced Sun   Underdeveloped Sun   Overdeveloped Sun

The three levels of development of Sun.

Sun

The Sanskrit word for the Sun is Surya, which means "that which radiates." The Sun mount reflects passion, conviction, courage, and creativity. Ideally, the Sun mount and finger indicate our potential to act from the heart, to extend ourselves spontaneously to others without looking for praise, recognition, or acknowledgment for what we do. Our passion for whatever it is we do is charismatic and may inspire others to pursue their own dreams.

An underdeveloped Sun indicates a reluctance to be exposed to the public. We do not have a strong enough passion to overcome our fear of failure. We need to practice taking risks in order to develop the confidence to fulfill our dreams. The Sun also stands for *atma*, the soul. Therefore, the case of an overdeveloped

Sun is slightly different from the other cases of overdeveloped mounts we have discussed so far. An individual with an overdeveloped Sun can be outstandingly creative and achieve greatness. The strength of our conviction, however, may lead us to have enormous expectations of others as well as of ourselves, which, in turn, could lead to misunderstanding and heartache. Also, there may be a temptation to become self-centered. Owing to the acclaim our brilliance may attract, we may begin to feel self-important and lose the original innocence that brought us the attention in the first place. We may use our charisma negatively to manipulate others. We need to retain a sense of humility, recognizing that our personal power is a gift to be shared with others.

Mercury

The Sanskrit word for Mercury is Buddh, which refers to enlightenment. Mercury relates to mental activity. It suggests curiosity and an interest in acquiring and relaying information. Like quicksilver, however, this mental activity needs the focus and structure of judgment. We need to discriminate between what is appropriate and what is superfluous.

The word *buddha*, meaning "enlightened one," shares the same root with Mercury, *Buddh*. Ideally, the finger and mount of Mercury indicate that, like the Buddha, we experience the joy that comes from the realization that the trinity of body, mind, and spirit is in fact the unity of soul. With this mental acuity, we can use our discriminating intelligence (*buddhi*), centered in the moment. We are able to focus on proper communication, through words or deeds, free from the doubts or expectations regarding the outcome that can serve as distractions.

The Mercury mount thus relates to communication and self-expression. As we begin to identify with the intuitive nature of our soul, and less with the intellect of the ego and physical desires, we develop a facility to express ourselves effortlessly to others. As we become less attached, we tend to take ourselves less seriously. We develop wit, quick thinking, and a sense of humor. Mercury also indicates the potential to develop our psychic and telepathic abilities. It may also denote healing and harmonizing capabilities.

An underdeveloped Mercury indicates reticence, naiveté, a lack of interest in our surroundings, and a reluctance to express ourselves in public. Since we lack curiosity and concentration, it may be difficult to learn or to remember details. We place a high value on tranquillity; however, we must guard against isolating ourselves from others.

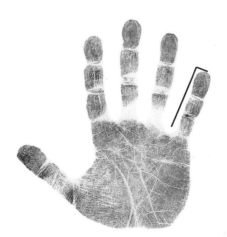 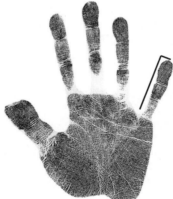 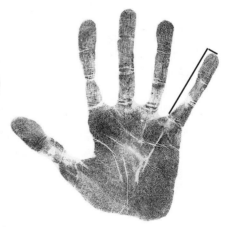

Balanced Mercury   Underdeveloped Mercury   Overdeveloped Mercury

The three levels of development of Mercury.

A well-developed mount of Mercury denotes a talent for playing an active role in the world. With this potential for positive communication and leadership, however, comes an equally great responsibility not to be led astray by the power of public recognition. An overdeveloped Mercury suggests the temptation to be too attached to the outer world at the expense of our inner harmony. Lacking discriminating intelligence, we may give undue attention to rumor and gossip, which we may accept as truth. In addition, we may be distracted by the possible fruits of our actions to the point where we disregard our conscience—our discriminating intelligence—and indulge in lying, cheating, or even stealing in order to acquire the things we

long for. We need to develop a sense of detachment and humility, like the Buddha.

Rahu and Ketu

Unlike the seven mounts that correspond to actual planetary bodies, the astrological zones corresponding to Rahu and its counterpart Ketu are the lunar nodes, referred to in palmistry and astrology as "shadow planets." They are the points of intersection of the Moon and Earth across the ecliptic path, when the Moon crosses the Sun's orbit—the points at which eclipses can occur. In the hand, they are the spaces left after all the other mounts have taken their place. They are opposite each other and are points of

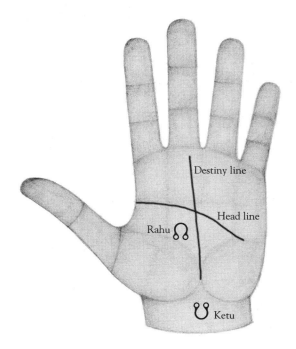

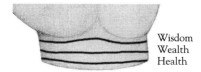

Rahu and Ketu are opposite each other in the hand. Rahu lies at the center of the palm and is the place
of intersection of the head and destiny lines. Ketu is located at the bottom of the palm and includes
the bracelets of the wrist—health, wealth, and wisdom.

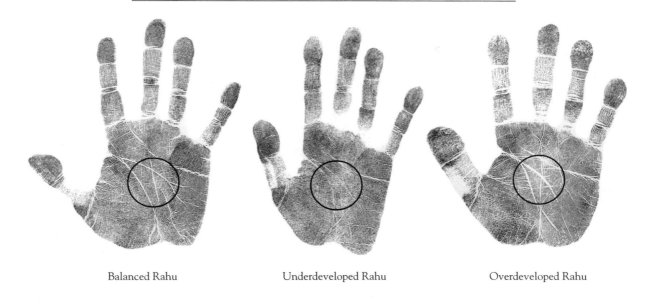

Balanced Rahu   Underdeveloped Rahu   Overdeveloped Rahu

The three levels of development of Rahu.

intersection for the major lines. As David Frawley says in *Astrology of the Seers*, "They show the potential for short-circuiting, as it were, our solar or lunar energies. They are thus very sensitive points that can cause repercussions in the total field of planetary forces."* Rahu relates to the present environment and Ketu to the sum total of all our past lives.

RAHU

Rahu refers to the point at which the Moon crosses the ecliptic to the north. In Vedic palmistry it is referred to as the Dragon's Head. Rahu is positioned at the center of the palm; it is bordered by the other mounts and is where the head and destiny lines intersect. An ideal mount

*David Frawley, *Astrology of the Seers* (Delhi, India: Motilal Banarsidass Publishers, 1990), 102.

of Rahu, which appears as a sort of valley surrounded by the other mounts, indicates that our immediate environment supports us in our life's journey. An underdeveloped Rahu, which creates too much of a ditch in the middle of the palm, suggests a loss of momentum that causes us to be overwhelmed by our environment; consequently, we are unable to make use of the possibilities available to us, and we need to reach out to those who can help motivate us. An overdeveloped Rahu, in which there is no hollow in the middle of the palm and the mount is flush with the rest of the hand, suggests that we are preoccupied with everyday concerns, which serve to distract us from discovering our long-term goals. We may have a tendency to be materialistic, and we need to recognize that our immediate environment is merely a step on a longer journey.

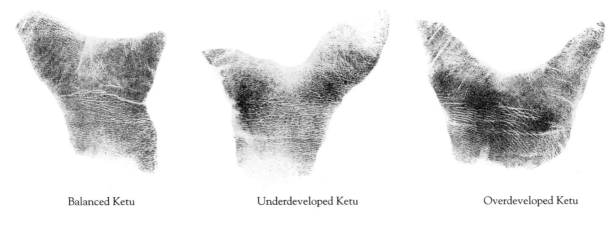

Balanced Ketu   Underdeveloped Ketu   Overdeveloped Ketu

The three levels of development of Ketu.

KETU

Ketu refers to the point at which the Moon crosses the ecliptic to the south. In Vedic palmistry it is referred to as the Dragon's Tail. Ketu is positioned at the bottom of the palm and includes the bracelets of the wrist; it is bordered by the Luna and Venus mounts, creating a cave.

Ketu indicates our past karma and its influences. The mount of Ketu is a record of the thoughts, ideals, hopes, and fears that we have carried from the past into the present life. The degree to which we have learned to integrate body, mind, and soul from previous incarnations is seen through a study of Ketu. This mount shows the strength of our first tentative steps in this life's journey. Consequently, the quality of this mount can indicate how our future may unfold. An ideal Ketu mount shows that we have assimilated the wisdom acquired in past lives and that we are ready to build upon that foundation to embrace new karma. An underdeveloped Ketu suggests an inhibition or fear of going forward in life; we wish to remain safe, holding onto the familiarity of past memories. We need to relinquish our fears, hurts, and insecurities to make room for new challenges in the present. An overdeveloped Ketu shows that we are too eager to rush headlong into new experiences without taking the time to digest and profit from past karmic lessons. We need to develop a proper sense of judgment, tempered with caution, before embarking on any new venture.

The relationship between Rahu and Ketu can be summed up by the well-known Sanskrit verse that tells us that "our present is the result of all our yesterdays, and the future depends on how well we live today."

The Pendulum Syndrome

An underdeveloped mount is usually an indication of either a lack of karmic experience or an overindulgence from the past in the area specific to the mount. For example, an underdeveloped Mercury mount may reflect a time in the past filled with public fame or notoriety. At present, therefore, we wish to avoid publicity and lead a quiet, undisturbed existence.

An overdeveloped mount suggests too great an emphasis on the area specific to the mount. For example, an overdeveloped Venus may indicate a predisposition to seek physical gratification. This can result in satiation, so that in the future, by way of reaction, we may have an underdeveloped Venus.

The study of palmistry provides us with the opportunity to anticipate this karmic pendulum swing. We can become aware of tendencies that pull us away from balanced behavior. This knowledge allows us to take conscious steps toward dealing with the imbalances in our lives, thereby minimizing the reactive effects of our actions. For example, an overdeveloped Sun alerts us to the possibility that we may become so attached to public acclaim that our original inspiration to share our talent becomes blocked.

Palmistry allows us to recognize that an underdeveloped mount does not simply require conscious positive steps to encourage more balanced behavior. It also invites us to look behind the lack of development to the attitude responsible for the excessive lifestyle that may have produced the pendulum swing. Only by dealing with both extremes can we achieve the ideal balance.

THE HAND DIVIDED INTO INNER AND OUTER WORLDS

One of the central concerns of palmistry is the extent to which our hand is balanced. We have discussed balance among the mounts. Now we shall look at the overall hand as a division into inner and outer worlds.

If we were to draw a line down the middle of the Saturn finger to the center of the wrist, the hand would be divided into the inner and outer worlds. The outer world consists of the zones of Sun, Mercury, Mars positive, and Luna. The inner world consists of the zones of Jupiter, Mars negative, Venus, and the thumb.

The mounts and fingers of the outer world indicate the qualities of our interaction with our environment. The outer world shows our public persona and our ability to communicate thoughts and ideas to the world. The mounts and fingers of the inner world indicate the

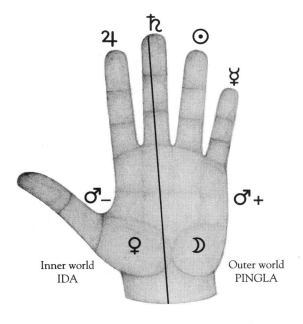

Drawing a line down the middle finger (Saturn) to the center of the wrist divides the hand into the inner and outer worlds.

qualities inherent in our inner aspirations and desires and our sense of individuality.

Our inner world is referred to as *ida*; it is negatively charged in nature, cooler, and more hidden. The outer world is referred to as *pingla*; it is positively charged, warmer, and more outgoing. Just as *ida* and *pingla* need to be balanced to act effectively, the inner and outer worlds of the hand need to be balanced before we can reliably trust our ability to reason and act objectively.

In Hindu texts, the area of Saturn is seen as the *sushumna*, or "mouth of God." In this hallowed spot *ida* and *pingla* first split from the neutral current in the spine to form the two aspects of our being: the emotional, receptive nature *(ida)* and the reasoning, outgoing nature *(pingla)*.

If we are overly *ida*, we can feel competent but not connected with our *pingla* energy. We

are cooler in temperament and dislike expressing ourselves in public. If the *pingla* side is more developed, we may be more outgoing and extroverted but also overbearing; we may be overly intense with no time to "smell the roses." We may lack a calm base for inner reflection and a sense of confidence to keep us cool.

Both worlds of the hand need to be balanced for us to feel complete. If we can achieve this, we feel confident, both within ourselves and in public. We express ourselves effortlessly. We no longer search for a missing part. The two aspects of ourselves may be distinct, but they are complementary and interconnected.

SATURN AND THE KALPNIC PATH

Another standard used to determine the degree of harmony in the hand is a comparison of the length of the Saturn finger to the length of the Kalpnic path.

Saturn is the middle finger and relates to thought. Physically, Saturn represents the spine, so its central location in the hand is significant. The finger lies between the positive and negative poles of the hand. It is the central point between our *ida* and *pingla* aspects and indicates our depth of thought and the degree to which we can be objective or neutral in our ability to be discerning.

The Kalpnic path crosses the mounts of Mars negative and Mars positive as well as the mount between these two, Rahu. The Kalpnic

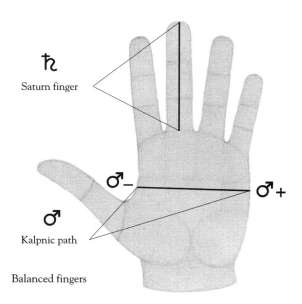

Ideally, the Saturn finger is equal to the length of the Kalpnic path which spans the area between ♂– and ♂+.

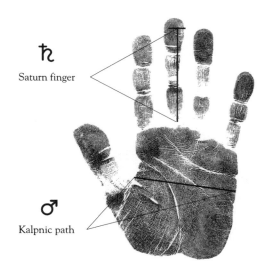

Saturn longer than the Kalpnic path.

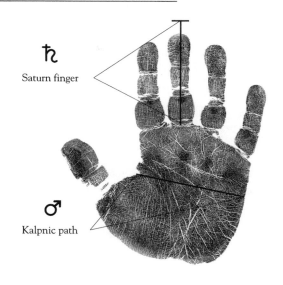

Saturn shorter than the Kalpnic path.

path joins physical energy (Mars negative) to mental energy (Mars positive) and indicates our sense of control within the present environment (Rahu). A balance between the two mounts of Mars indicates an abundance of energy that is not dissipated in negative emotion or feelings of helplessness. When the length of the Saturn finger equals the length of the Kalpnic path, our energy is well directed; the wise contemplative judgment related to Saturn gives stability to the volatility of our nervous and mental energies.

In Sanskrit, knowledge or wisdom (connected to Saturn) is called *gyana*, while *guna* denotes virtue. A balance between Saturn and the Kalpnic path means *gyana* has become *guna*, thought has become virtue. We have taken static knowledge (Saturn) and learned how to animate it (Mars). Internal energy is being expressed ex-

ternally. We are relating successfully to the world.

When *gyana*, or knowledge alone (too much Saturn), remains interiorized and stagnant, we may demonstrate an overly serious, silent, and reserved nature. But too wide a Mars galaxy (too long a Kalpnic path) in proportion to Saturn indicates that we may be too exteriorized, or overly active and talkative without the guidance of discrimination and proper judgment.

In the example showing a longer Saturn, we see that the individual has a great deal of knowledge, but this wisdom is not well supported by either the nervous system or the body. Most of the energy remains in the mind, so the individual is unable to act on this knowledge. *Gyana*, knowledge, is not supported by the fire of action. Therefore, *guna*, or virtue, has not yet been achieved.

In the example showing a shorter Saturn

we see a strong nervous system, but it is unsupported by knowledge and reliable discernment. The energy functions more on a physical plane, reflecting a tendency toward pleasure and thrill seeking. The *guna* attributes are unable to flourish. An overdeveloped Mars without adequate support from Saturn means that although we may be energetic and dynamic, we don't have enough discrimination, wisdom, and discipline to reach our goals.

THE MAJOR
AND MINOR LINES

The features of the hand reflect the process of our karmic evolution. The mounts, which are the foundation for the lines and signs of the hand, represent our soul or superconscious nature. Lines running vertically indicate our conscious awareness of ourselves as spiritual beings. Lines running horizontally across the palm reflect our degree of rootedness in a physical, incarnate state.

In Vedic palmistry, the lines on the hand are classified as major and minor. The major lines— the heart line, the head line, and the life line— reflect the subconscious or, in Sanskrit terminology, *awachetan*. Our emotions, our intellect, and our body are the primary tools of existence. They enable us to function as individuals but limit us to a sensory perception of reality. This limitation is manifest in the horizontal nature of these lines. In other words, a life lived purely at the subconscious or instinctive level will prove a barrier to karmic evolution.

The minor lines—destiny, Mercury, and Sun—reflect the conscious or, in Sanskrit terminology, *chetan mastishk*. These lines represent the degree to which we are able to use our physical, mental, and emotional attributes to reconnect with our divine nature. This creative impulse to break free of our physical limitations is shown in the vertical nature of the lines, as we move beyond day-to-day existence toward the freedom of universal consciousness.

The Major Lines

There are three principal lines in the hand. In Hindu terminology they are known as *jeevan rekha* (life line), *mastak rekha* (head line), and *hradaya rekha* (heart line).

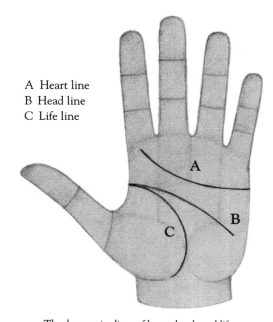

A Heart line
B Head line
C Life line

The three major lines of heart, head, and life.

The heart line shows how we respond emotionally. The head line indicates our ability to make decisions based on reason. The life line reflects the quality of our physical life. The basic human constituents of body, mind, and emotion provide the means for us to interact with our social environment. Our subconscious, indicated by the major lines, links our conscious waking state to that of our superconscious, the soul.

The major lines indicate deep-rooted patterns showing how we behave in different situations. For example, if someone yells at us, do we react? Do we get angry, fearful, or defensive; or do we hold our ground with a view to resolving the issue? When we remain calm under all conditions, we exhibit *buddhi* consciousness. When our behavior is governed primarily by a reaction to the behavior of others, we exhibit *manas* behavior. As we learn to remain objective, we begin to see positive changes in the major lines of the hand.

The Trinity of Sattwa, Rajas, and Tamas Reflected in the Three Major Lines

We see the trinity of *sattwa*, *rajas*, and *tamas* in the three major lines. The heart line is *sattwic*, the head line is *rajasic*, and the life line is *tamasic*. Each of the major lines can reveal unity or disharmony in the *guna* it represents. For example, the heart line is in the *sattwic* realm; however, if we are not expressing our soul-self through *buddhi*, we may be selfish and remote instead of loving and generous.

The head line in the *rajasic* realm becomes the link between our soul (heart line) and our

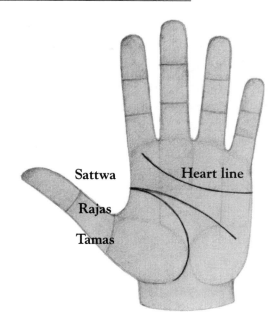

The heart line is situated in the top third portion of the palm and is sattwic *in nature.*

body (life line). It is essential that our mind be calm and focused in order to make this connection integral. The life line is located in the *tamasic* realm and relates to how we express our physical nature; while it can be the source of attachment and personal gratification, it can also be our means of expressing love to others selflessly.

The Heart Line

The heart line is situated in the top third portion of the palm and is *sattwic* in nature. Ideally, the heart line should span the top four mounts, originating in Jupiter and ending in Mercury. Drawing upon the energy of all four *sattwic* mounts, the heart line reflects the idealistic and high-minded aspect of our being, which is closest to spirit. We express the spirit-self through our emotions—ideally, love or devotion, characteristic of *buddhi*. When we are in tune with our soul-self, we are naturally generous and accepting. Ideal love is unconditional. It transcends logic and thinking. Our emotions, however, are often influenced by personal complexities involving the mind *(manas)*. When we start to feel "I need this," "I deserve that," "I expect this," we filter love through the mind. Our emotions become a liability when love becomes self-centered rather than all-embracing.

The heart line also signifies the physical condition of the actual heart organ. Life events, most particularly those relating to interpersonal relationships, also register on this major line.

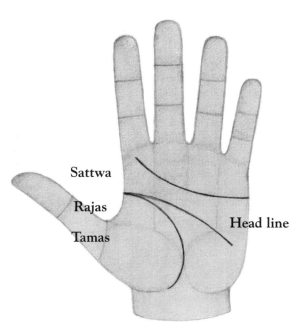

Sattwa

Rajas

Tamas

Head line

The head line is situated in the middle third of the palm and is rajasic *in nature.*

The Head Line

The head line is situated in the middle third of the palm and is *rajasic* in nature. Ideally, the head line travels across the Kalpnic path, forming a bridge between the inner and outer worlds of the palm. This connection provides us with the courage of conviction to believe in our inner aspirations and ideas. The head line reflects our reasoning abilities and intellect. As such, our mind can be our best ally or worst enemy. Ideally, the head line indicates that we have the potential to be objective, that we can "weigh the facts" in a situation and make impartial decisions. We understand the consequences of our actions. We are intelligent and visionary and can have long-range goals and ambitions.

Our thinking, however, is often influenced by personal needs, desires, and expectations. In situations that directly affect us we may have great difficulty maintaining our objectivity. Our thinking may be ego-centered, we may tend to convince ourselves that it is valid, and our behavior will reflect our subjective thinking. Our analysis of the situation will be limited by our self-preoccupation, and our decisions will be influenced by self-justification. The mind, then, can be a vehicle for making the superconscious apparent at a conscious level, which is *buddhi*; or the mind can limit our perception of reality to that which is defined through our senses, which is *manas*.

The head line also signifies the physical condition of the brain. Specific life events, particularly those that affect our mental health and psychological outlook, also register on this major line.

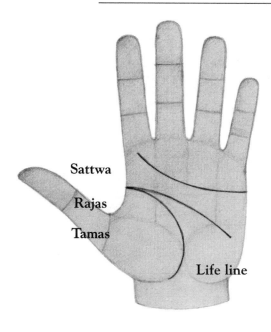

The life line is located in the bottom third of the hand and is tamasic *in nature.*

The Life Line

The life line is located in the bottom third of the hand. It relates to our *tamasic* nature. The location of this line in the densest realm of the palm reflects the degree of our *prana* or life force, which is evident in our breathing. According to Eastern tradition, the first breath, taken at birth, is what defines us as a separate physical body. The life line indicates matters of health and longevity by showing how appropriately we manage and expend our life force. When we are excitable and nervous, our breathing is rapid and shallow. When we are calm and controlled, our breathing is slow and deep. An ancient proverb states, "We have a predetermined number of breaths to sustain life." We should be careful not to waste a single breath.

The life line also shows our attitude and potential to flow with or against the current of life. Do we see life as a constant challenge (*manas*) that we consistently confront—exhausting ourselves in the process? Or do we use energy wisely and deal with difficult circumstances? In the latter, we recognize that life is a complex, often challenging maze that can provide endless opportunities for self-understanding (*buddhi*).

The life line indicates our potential to relate harmoniously with those around us. It also yields information about our physical well-being, including the condition of the nervous system and our degree of stamina. This line reveals the extent of our enthusiasm for life, how willing we are to undertake challenges. From a spiritual viewpoint, the life line indicates our capacity for self-control. Are the

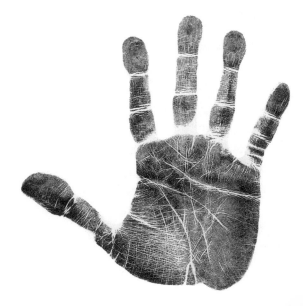

In this example, the three major lines are balanced, reflecting harmony of body, mind, and soul.

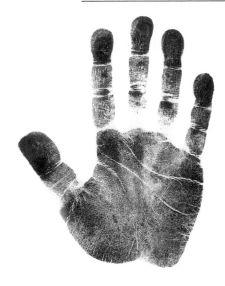

In this example, we find a disproportionately strong head line in comparison with the other two major lines. This individual's brilliant intellect is not supported by equally long heart and life lines. The mind has become all-important, leading to a way of life that is out of touch with the needs of others and thus appearing to be self-centered.

In this case, we find a disproportionately strong heart line in comparison with the other two major lines. This individual's loving nature is not supported by equally long head and life lines. Instead of the heart being supported by proper judgment, feelings have become so important that this individual is drawn into relationships that are potentially life threatening.

senses a means to spiritual growth, or are they an end in themselves?

Our Subconscious: Harmony in the Major Lines

All three of the major lines should be round in nature and not crossed by interference lines, islanded, or blocked in any way. They should be equally strong, deep, and long. When they are balanced in this manner, they reflect harmony in body, mind, and soul.

The head line, by its location between the other two major lines, creates a neutral zone or boundary between *sattwa* and *tamas*. For this reason, the head line is referred to as *rajas*, "king." By the discriminating power of *buddhi*,

the mind in the *rajasic* zone is able to create harmony between the physical self in the *tamasic* realm (life line) and our spirit in the *sattwic* realm (heart line). Through *manas*, however, our mind can keep us separated from our spiritual nature, disrupting the trinity of body, mind, and soul. Just as Aum symbolizes the manifestation of Parambrahma, the One, through the trinity of Brahma, Vishnu, and Shiva, the ideal formation of the heart, head, and life lines in the hand manifests the integration of the *gunas*.

The Quadrangle

The quadrangle, sometimes referred to as "the landing strip of the angels," is a significant indicator of mental and emotional harmony. It

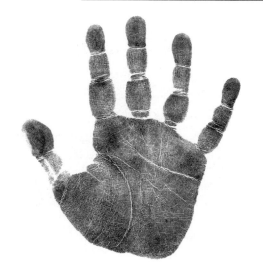

In this case, we find a disproportionately strong life line in comparison with the other two major lines. This individual's preoccupation with living "the good life" without regard to the long-term consequences can lead to inappropriate behavior and a life unconcerned with social responsibility.

make decisions. But when we achieve a balance between reason and feeling, one part of us no longer pulls the other out of alignment. Equilibrium brings with it peace and serenity, and in this state, we are more receptive to "angel visits" in the form of good friends, wise teachers, visionary dreams, intuitions, and sound advice.

The Minor Lines: Our Conscious Self

In addition to the three major lines there are many other significant lines and signs. Three of the most important minor lines in the hand are the destiny line, the Sun line, and the Mercury line. In Sanskrit they are known as *Karma rekha*, *Surya rekha*, and *Buddh rekha*.

is made up of the head and heart lines, which represent the two sides of our nature: the heart being the positive pole (relating to feelings), and the head the negative pole (reason). The heart and head lines should be equal in length and should not touch, as any joining or overlapping indicates a short circuit similar to that in electricity. Ideally, these lines should have a slight tendency toward an hourglass shape, with the distance between them neither too narrow nor too wide.

It takes effort to balance these two aspects of the self. A head line that overpowers the heart line may indicate a tendency to rationalize our feelings. If the heart line overpowers the head line, we may be emotionally biased when we

The quadrangle is a significant indicator of mental and emotional harmony.

The minor lines reflect our conscious awareness. They indicate how connected we are to our deepest soul nature or how distracted we are by the changing environment around us. These lines indicate how we experience life on a conscious level and reflect our thoughts and attitudes, as well as the behaviors that we exhibit.

The minor lines create a channel for the conscious expression of our superconscious (mounts) and subconscious (major lines). They act as an interface for our soul to express itself in our everyday conscious behavior. Their presence indicates a conscious awareness and attunement (*buddhi*) to our deepest self. When these lines are crossed by interference lines, are broken, or are missing, however, the conscious connection with our soul nature is disrupted. We become overidentified with the demands of our environment and lose our sense of inner peace.

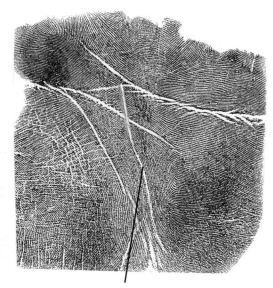

Destiny line

The destiny line indicates that we have a conscious awareness of life's purpose.

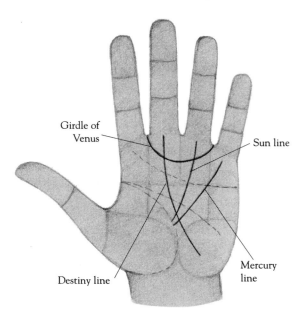

Girdle of Venus

Sun line

Destiny line

Mercury line

The minor lines reflect our conscious awareness.

The formation of the minor lines indicates the degree to which we are able to integrate our deeper, intuitive soul-self. We recognize that our everyday thoughts and behavior can have positive or negative effects on those around us. We become aware of the importance of being responsible, helpful, and loving in our daily activities. We learn to transcend the individual in favor of the universal—a characteristic of *buddhi* consciousness. Ignorance of our soul nature, however, indicates that our conscious choices in life are bound by personal desires based on *manas* or ego consciousness.

The Destiny Line

The destiny line runs vertically up toward the Saturn mount through Rahu, which is located in the center of the palm. This line, like a clearly outlined path, indicates that we have been born to journey through life with some purpose. As such, it relates to career potential. Our immediate environment, reflected by Rahu, enables us to experience a wide spectrum of circumstances through which we are challenged to grow and evolve. We can experience life spontaneously through a succession of random events that just happen (manas), or we can choose to recognize that life is a sequence of purposeful events (buddhi). The destiny line indicates that we have a conscious awareness of life's purpose and that embedded within each experience is a choice.

An ideal destiny line is deep, long, and straight, without breaks or interference. In geometry, the shortest distance between two points is a straight line. The destiny line indicates that

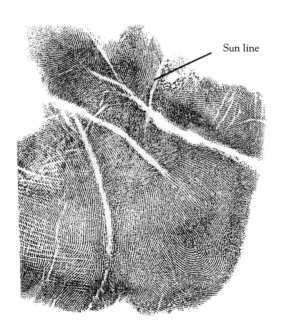

The Sun line has also been called the "line of success."

our inherent potential to be focused, disciplined, and structured can act like a straightedge, guiding our karmic unfoldment from birth to death along a true and undeviating path.

Sun Line

The Sun line runs vertically up the palm and through the Sun mount in the *sattwic* realm of the palm. This mount relates to *atma*, the soul, which is a spark of the universal light. As such, the Sun line indicates our conscious awareness of the infinite potential within us. We may be inspired by our heart's desire that may, at first, appear to be an impossible dream; however, by tapping into the creative energy of the Sun, we can make it happen. Our example may also inspire others.

The Sun line has also been called the "line of success." Each of us, however, views success differently. For some, it may mean the acquisition of material wealth; for some it may mean prestige and status in the community; for others it may mean a life devoted to the service of others. The degree to which we are able to sublimate our ego in the universal determines how appropriately we are using our Sun energy. For example, Mother Teresa reached out to the sick and dying in the streets of Calcutta, drawing volunteers from all over the world (buddhi). She regarded what she did as perfectly ordinary—a humble act of charity. Others consider her work a miracle. Another person in the same situation might have been caught up in the fame and public recognition (manas), which would have distanced them from the very people they were trying

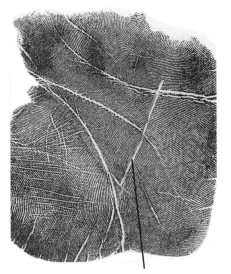

Mercury line

*The Mercury line is the line
of self-expression.*

to help. Ideally, then, the Sun line indicates our capacity for integrity, commitment, and devotion.

Mercury Line

The Mercury line is found running diagonally from the life line, in the *tamasic* realm, through the head line and the heart line up into the Mercury mount, the *sattwic* realm. It reveals our ability to focus our attention unimpeded by reason, emotion, or physical concerns. The Mercury line is the line of self-expression. It indicates our potential to apply our particular talents effortlessly. An accomplished dancer can give a brilliant performance and, only afterward, realize that she has torn a ligament. During the actual performance, the dancer was so involved in communicating her art that space and time were transcended: the pain did not exist until the dance ended. This focus that the Mercury line suggests allows us to be caught up in the joy and spontaneity of "the moment" (*buddhi*). Conversely, a dancer can be so distracted by a child crying in the audience that she is unable to give a good performance (*manas*).

Sometimes, this line is referred to as the "line of health." It is not an indication of the state of our health, but rather the degree to which any infirmity or illness, whether

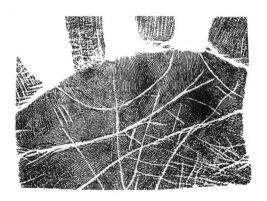

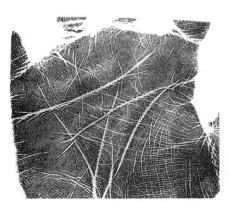

*In the example on the left, we see equal development of the three minor lines of destiny, Sun,
and Mercury. In the example on the right, there are strong Mercury and destiny lines;
the individual should be encouraged to develop the Sun line.*

physical, mental, or emotional, hinders our self-expression. A break or interference on this line may indicate the origin of possible health issues.

Our Conscious:
Harmony in the Minor Lines

As is the case with the major lines, optimally the minor lines should be equal in strength. This is especially true of the destiny, Sun, and Mercury lines, which together signify that our purpose is going to be fulfilled with ease of expression. For example, a strong destiny line without the support of the Sun and Mercury lines indicates that our hard work is not rewarded by a feeling of satisfaction. A strong Sun line without the support of the destiny and Mercury lines indicates that we are content with our good fortune but lack a real sense of direction. A strong Mercury line without the support of the destiny and Sun lines indicates that we are able to communicate with others freely but without purpose.

Miscellaneous Minor Lines
GIRDLE OF VENUS

The girdle of Venus forms an arc that extends from the junction of the Jupiter and Saturn fingers and continues toward the junction of the Sun and Mercury fingers. The location of the girdle of Venus above the heart line in the *sattwic* realm indicates that we feel deeply and that our sentiments can be attuned to spirit. We are able to translate our sensory impressions into some form of creative expression that can touch the hearts of others. An improperly formed girdle of Venus, however, indicates that we may have difficulty channeling our feelings. We may be passionate and intense yet unable to find a creative outlet for our feelings. This may result in escapist or unpredictable behavior.

VIA LASCIVIA

In contrast to the girdle of Venus is the *via lascivia*, which forms a bridge between the Luna and Venus mounts in the *tamas* realm of the

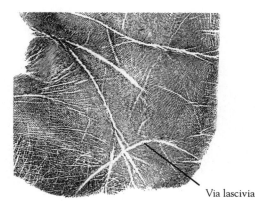

Girdle of Venus

The girdle of Venus indicates great sensitivity and artistic expression.

Via lascivia

The via lascivia *suggests that we are preoccupied with the gratification of physical desires.*

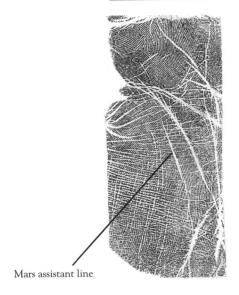

Mars assistant line

The Mars assistant line indicates our receptivity to supportive relationships.

hand. The presence of this line suggests that we are preoccupied with the gratification of physical desires. The downward-turning nature of this line indicates a need to rechannel the senses. First, we must recognize that our preoccupation with fulfilling our physical desires may stem from a spiritual or emotional emptiness. Our attempt

to fill this void at a physical level often leads to obsessive-compulsive behavior. When we see that sensory gratification is temporary and we have become trapped in a self-destructive cycle, we can break the pattern by finding more appropriate and fulfilling endeavors. For example, someone with an eating disorder can learn to control their obsession with food by understanding the source of their inner hunger. They may need professional help in order to develop alternate means of nurturing themselves.

THE MARS ASSISTANT LINE

The Mars assistant line originates in the mount of Mars negative, our masculine aspect. It runs parallel to the life line, terminating in the mount of Venus, our feminine aspect. Forming a connection between these two mounts, the Mars assistant line indicates that there is conscious recognition of these two aspects of ourselves. We accept our aggressive, active qualities as coexisting equally with our sensitive, yielding nature. This perception of our male/female persona allows us to be more at

Union lines

The union line indicates our willingness to make a commitment to another person.

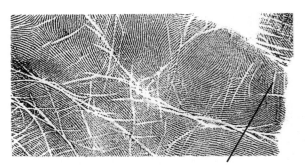

Children line

The children lines indicate the desire and potential to have children.

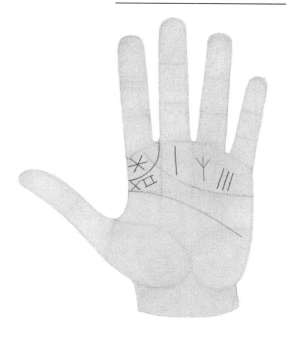

*Lines and signs of wisdom on any mount show that
we are developing the positive attributes associated with that
particular astrological zone.*

horizontal, which usually indicates struggle. A relationship provides us with the opportunity both to put down roots and to develop greater spiritual freedom by transcending our ego through love.

Children lines rise vertically or diagonally from the union line. They indicate the desire and potential to have children. Unlike the horizontal union line, which stresses merging and rootedness, the upward nature of the children lines indicates both the creation of offspring and the eventual "letting go" as the children grow up and search to establish their own roots.

Lines and Signs of Wisdom

In addition to the specific positive minor lines described above, there are other lines and signs of wisdom found throughout the hand that indicate the degree of our receptivity to higher knowledge. Their presence on any mount shows

ease with ourselves. Consequently, we attract supportive people into our life. Our relationships are based on genuine love and mutual respect rather than codependency.

THE UNION AND CHILDREN LINES

The presence of lines and signs on the Mercury mount indicates the desire or need for relationships that provide opportunities for karmic evolution.

The union line is located horizontally on the Mercury mount. It originates on the percussion of the hand (the outside edge of the palm). The presence of a union line indicates our willingness to make a commitment to another person. Of significance is the fact that the union line is one of the few minor lines that is

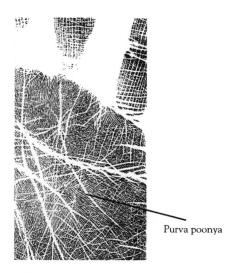

Purva poonya

The purva poonya *line translates as
good karma from the past.*

that we are developing the positive attributes associated with that particular astrological zone. The exact interpretation of any of these activity signs depends on their location, their formation, and on the quality of mount where they are found. They may take the form of crosses, grills, tridents, caves, kites, flags, and squares, which many of us have on our hands.

PURVA POONYA

The *purva poonya* line translates as good karma from the past. It originates on the mount of Mars positive, the repository of past deeds. Traveling upward through the heart line to the Sun mount, the *purva poonya* line indicates good fortune. Because it connects these two mounts, the *purva poonya* line indicates continuity between our passion and commitment to past ventures and our present success. We may also attract old friends who can support us.

THE RING OF SOLOMON

The ring of Solomon, named after the wise king Solomon, forms an arc on the Jupiter mount. Jupiter is also called *Guru* or "dispeller of darkness," which implies that the ideal expression of this mount is expansive, tolerant, and illuminating. The presence of the ring of Solomon suggests that, rather than pursuing our ambitions for personal gain, we recognize that the prosperity of others is equally important to us. Ideally, people in professions such as psychology, political leadership, and the judicial system have this sign.

Ring of Solomon

The ring of Solomon forms an arc around the Jupiter mount and denotes wisdom.

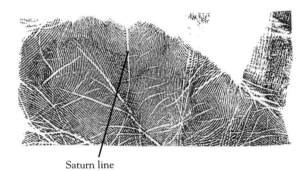

Saturn line

The Saturn line reflects our love of truth.

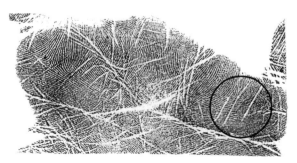

Healing stigmata

The healing stigmata denote empathy and healing abilities.

THE SATURN LINE

The Saturn line, which is also referred to as the "line of truth" or the "love of God line," is located vertically on the Saturn mount, connecting the *sattwa*, *rajas*, and *tamas* worlds within the Saturn mount. This line indicates the extent to which we search for truth and meaning in life; it indicates we are willing to accept criticism from those we love and trust.

THE HEALING STIGMATA

The mount and finger of Mercury relate to our communication ability, that is, how well we listen and respond to others. The presence of healing stigmata reveals that we have perfected our listening skills and can hear beyond what is being said. In the East, they denote telepathic abilities. Deeply in tune with the feelings of others, we are able to offer comfort. The healing stigmata consist of three parallel diagonal lines on the Mercury mount. These lines relate to the three *gunas*, *sattwa*, *rajas*, and *tamas*. Their diagonal placement suggests we are in the process of perfecting the qualities related to the Mercury mount. Due to our empathy, we are able to put aside our personal needs and desires as we respond to the pain of others. People in the health care professions often have these lines; however, they are also found in anyone who uses their communicative abilities in a healing manner.

Interference Lines

The negative counterpart to the lines and signs of wisdom are the lines of interference, which

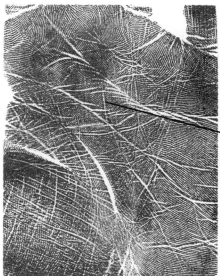

Destiny line growing stronger after the interference line

Destiny line terminating with the interference line at the head line

Lines of interference reflect the fact that we are encountering difficulties in our lives. In the top example, the person is overcoming the difficulties he is faced with and becoming stronger as a result.
In the bottom example, the individual is being overwhelmed by the challenges he is facing. In the top example, the destiny line is stronger after the interference line; in the bottom example, the destiny line is weaker after the interference.

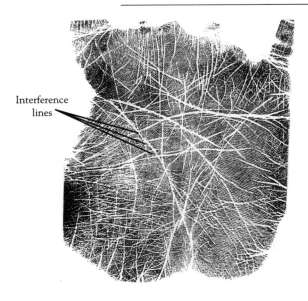

Interference
lines

*Interference lines originating from
Mars negative suggest difficulties stemming
from early childhood.*

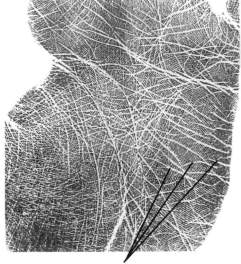

Interference lines

*Interference lines originating from Mars positive indicate
our worry about fulfilling our responsibilities.*

may be warning signals of frustration, anguish, and other nonproductive emotions. Contrary to the positive minor lines of wisdom that run vertically on the palm, interference lines usually run horizontally. They represent obstructions to the upward, transcending lines of destiny, Sun, and Mercury. Referred to as blessings in disguise, these lines reflect tests and challenges. In order to gauge how we approach these tests to our nature, we must check to see if the minor lines are stronger or weaker after an interference line has crossed them.

INTERFERENCE LINES FROM MARS NEGATIVE

Interference lines originating from Mars negative run horizontally on the palm. These lines suggest difficulties stemming from early childhood, either from within the family or from cir-

Interference lines

*Interference lines originating from Venus suggest
difficulties stemming from the immediate environment.*

cumstances in the immediate environment. Lines that stop short of the life line indicate resolution of early emotional disturbances. However, interference lines that cross the life line or extend to the head or heart lines suggest that we need to deal with these early issues; otherwise, they may continue to affect our health—physically, mentally, and emotionally.

INTERFERENCE LINES ON MARS POSITIVE

Horizontal lines on the percussion of the hand, on the mount of Mars positive, are a common phenomenon. They indicate our concern with day-to-day responsibilities and may be a sign of energy depletion. We may expend energy in worry rather than directing our efforts to meet challenges. Upward-turning lines suggest that we are able to accept our responsibilities without being overwhelmed by them.

INTERFERENCE LINES FROM VENUS

Horizontal lines that originate in the mount of Venus and do not extend beyond the life line are lines of self-expression and are considered positive features. When these lines cross the life line, however, they reveal difficulties relating to circumstances that we attract rather than inherit from our family. These obstacles provide us with the opportunity to develop strength, perseverance, and understanding in our dealings with others. For this reason they are sometimes referred to as "blessings in disguise."

RING OF SATURN

This line encircles the mount of Saturn. It indicates a tendency to harbor introspective

Ring of Saturn

The ring of Saturn indicates a propensity to be overly pensive to the point of being isolated from others.

thoughts, and consequently, we may become pessimistic, moody, and despondent.

Harmony Reflected by the Presence of Wisdom Lines

A number of markings—for example, crosses, squares, tridents, and stars—may indicate positive qualities, depending on their locations. We refer to these auspicious signs as wisdom markings. They show that we have developed greater maturity and reliability and are becoming more consciously aware of others. The presence of wisdom lines and signs, together with a minimum of interference lines, is a barometer indicating the depth of our inner peace and happiness.

The Balance of Mounts and Major and Minor Lines

The mounts provide the ground upon which the major and minor lines travel. A good indicator of harmony among the mounts is the state of the lines. Ideally, both major and minor lines should

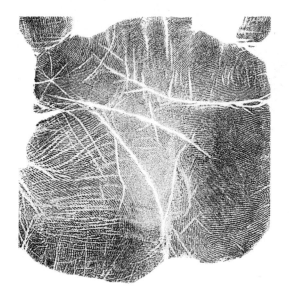 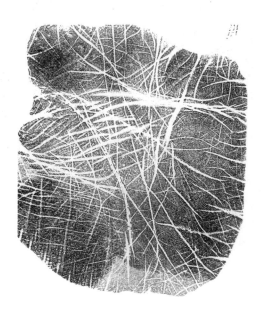

In the example on the left, we see the presence of wisdom signs; in the example on the right, the individual is facing many obstructions.

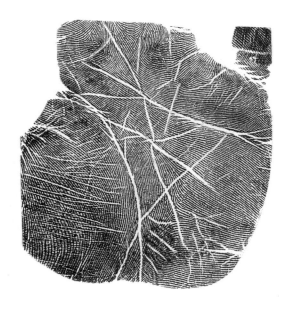 

On the left, we see the minor lines equal in strength to the major lines. This shows that the individual is conscious of his unique individuality and can express it effortlessly.
On the right, the minor lines are weaker, indicating the individual is more tentative, distracted, and not fully aware or conscious of developing his inner resources.

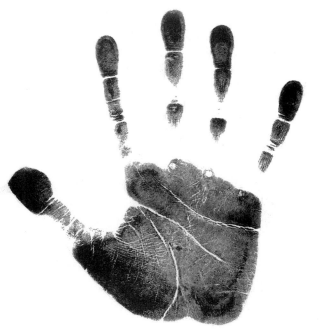 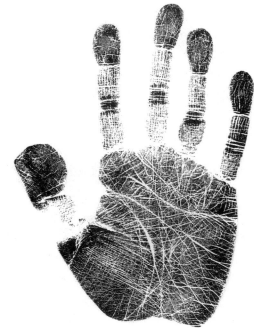

The presence of the three major lines alone.   *The presence of too many minor lines.*

be of equal length, depth, and intensity. When the lines and mounts are balanced, our superconscious is free, unhindered by conscious or subconscious obstructions.

The conscious mind, represented by the minor lines, reflects awareness of our inner talents. The minor lines show how in touch we are with our subconscious and superconscious. When we are preoccupied by the circumstances and events around us, we may lose contact with our inner self. Our preoccupation will be reflected by a busy network of minor lines obscuring the major lines and the mounts beneath them. Since our external environment is constantly changing, the minor lines are often seen as being in flux. Remaining peaceful in the midst of change is reflected in the minor

lines being equal in strength to the major lines, allowing the energy of the mounts to be expressed through them. The minor lines act as a barometer to show how connected we are with our deeper self while facing everyday challenges.

Deeply rooted convictions are not easy to modify. Thus change in the major lines takes a great deal of time and effort. Changes in the formation of the mounts are even more challenging, as they reflect our superconscious nature.

Major Lines Alone

The presence of only the major lines in our hands indicates that our life unfolds as a series of events that simply happen to us. We enjoy the positive ones and endure those that are difficult. We may lead a mechanical existence, unaware of our potential for expressing the depth of our emotions and intentions. We may have the feeling that, although we have rich resources and capabilities, we have no outlet for expression. Naturally we will feel frustrated or disconnected from our inner capabilities, as if we were sleepwalking through life.

Too Many Minor Lines

Too many minor lines are like weeds in a garden, distorting our expression. The presence of too many minor lines means we are overwhelmed by our present situation and can be distracted by circumstances, runaway thoughts, whims, and ideas. A preoccupation with the details of day-to-day living may make it impossible for us to tap into our inner resources. The minor lines, however, register positive changes readily as we become more conscious of our capabilities. Changes in these lines are often visible in as little as three months.

In conclusion, minor lines show to what extent we are able to delve into the superconscious in order to enrich our consciousness. The presence of major lines alone, without support from the minor lines, means we lead a more mechanical existence, whereas the presence of minor lines reveals awakened consciousness. When the mounts are "raw"—that is, coarse in texture and without any lines—we have not yet tapped the creative potential inherent in that mount. The absence of lines on the mount indicates that we are not consciously putting to good use the latent characteristics of that mount.

3

Which Hand Should We Consult?

Scientists refer to the human body as a bilaterally symmetrical organism, each half of which has one leg, one arm, a hand, an eye, an ear, and so on. Our two halves are not as symmetrical as they appear, however. For example, neurological studies have revealed that the two hemispheres of the brain specialize in different psychological functions. The right hemisphere is primarily the seat of emotions, intuition, artistic ability, and spatial perception. The left hemisphere is largely responsible for linear reasoning, logic, and language. Researchers have also shown that even the two halves of the human face, which at first glance seem identical, actually contain subtle but appreciable differences in structure and expression.

Palmistry examines the link between the thought patterns located in each hemisphere of the brain and the structural patterns on the corresponding hand.

BRAIN/HAND CORRELATION

Neurology provides clear evidence that the left hemisphere of the brain actually controls the right side of the body, owing to the crossing of nerve fibers. Therefore, for most people, the left side of the brain,

A

B

We often think of people's faces as symmetrical, but as these photographs reveal, the left and right sides of our faces are distinctly different. Look at what happens in figure B when one side of an individual's face is taken and "flipped" to create the other side. The result is often not what one would expect!

which controls the right hand, is dominant. For left-handed individuals, the right brain hemisphere is dominant. Palmistry examines the link between the thought patterns located in each hemisphere and the structural patterns on the corresponding hand.

In terms of function, one side of the body is generally predominant. The right side is stron-

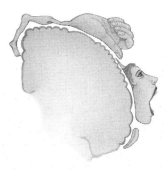

Dr. Wilder Penfield, a Canadian brain surgeon, identified the areas of the brain responsible for the transfer of information to the various parts of the body by means of electrical stimulation of the motor section of the cerebral cortex. It is interesting to see how large an area of the cortex is linked to the thumb, the fingers, and the hand.

ger than the left in approximately 90 percent of the human population. This means that with most people, the right hand is the dominant hand; it has a firmer grasp (that is, greater muscle development), greater dexterity and coordination, and greater responsiveness. The dominant hand is the hand we naturally give preference to for the finer, more specialized motor skills like writing, drawing, sewing, cutting, and so forth.

WHICH HAND SHOULD WE CONSULT?

Because writing requires great attention and dexterity, the hand we write with is considered our active hand. The active hand represents our present resolve and the goals we want to achieve. The inactive hand reflects all that we have inherited from the past, such as old behavior patterns, thoughts, desires, and attitudes. By comparing the active and inactive hands, we can see if any old, unwanted behavior patterns are being replaced by more positive ones. Study of the two hands together is necessary. We may have positive resolve to change for the better, as seen by the active hand; however, we must also be aware of any potentially self-defeating patterns we may have carried with us from the past, as shown by our inactive hand.

Palmists study both hands in order to understand more about the thought habits of the past and how these can affect our will to change in the present. The hands portray the struggles we experience in working to overcome self-imposed limitations. When we compare our hands, we gain an understanding of where we are coming from and where we are headed.

What Do We Mean by the Past?

The ancient texts of *samudrik shastra* state that the inactive hand reflects all the memories, desires, attitudes, and habits that we have accumulated over the last three lifetimes. But for any of us who find it difficult to relate to the concept of reincarnation, the past can be regarded simply as the sum total of our genetic makeup inherited in the form of memories or behavior from our ancestors. Time is relative. No matter how long it takes to form a habit—whether a month or a lifetime—the inactive hand shows the accumulation of all those character qualities that have made us who we are today. These include inherited traits, which can skip a generation and perhaps reappear later in a grandchild.

With regard to our inactive and active hands, we can also wonder at what point the past ends and the present begins. According to *samudrik* texts, we enter an astral realm at the time of death following our immediate past life. During this astral existence, we have the opportunity to review our life and formulate new resolutions. Unencumbered by the pressures and preoccupations of earthly existence, we are free to assess our accomplishments. Did they leave us with a sense of satisfaction? Did we realize our potentials? What effect did our behavior have upon others? Were we instrumental in helping others get in touch with deeper aspects of themselves? What do we still wish to accomplish?

When we are born, the lines and signs of our active hand reflect these new resolutions. The sum total of our attitudes, thoughts, and behavior is shown in the features of the inactive hand at the time of our birth. As our life unfolds, the lines and signs change to reflect the degree to which we have been able to act upon our resolutions.

Evolutionary Progress: Our Active and Inactive Hands

Ideally, the hands reflect an evolutionary progress taking place from the inactive to the active hand. Cases of regression are infrequent. By comparing the inactive hand to the active one, we can see to what degree we have advanced in depth and refinement of character.

The active hand reveals resolutions for the next three lifetimes. Thus, it acts as a screen

Signs of evolutionary progress in the active hand

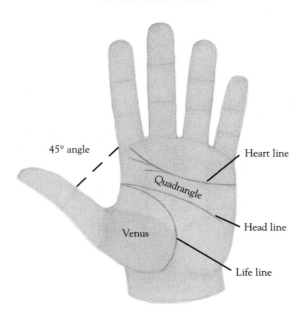

45° angle

Quadrangle

Heart line

Venus

Head line

Life line

Many factors must be studied to determine whether progress is being made from the inactive to the active hand. Some signs to look for in the active hand are improvement in the thumb angle, the formation of the quadrangle, the major lines, and the mount of Venus.

upon which we project images of changes we would like to see in ourselves and the way we live. Habits developed over many incarnations are not easily modified, however. Therefore, the patterns of thought and behavior reflected in the inactive hand are likely to perpetuate themselves, despite a good resolve to change for the better. There must be a supportive environment for changes to take root, as well as adequate time to put intentions into practice, lest the inactive-hand traits reemerge in our conscious expression.

Many factors must be studied to determine whether progress is being made from the inactive to the active hand. Normally, the thumb in the active hand is stronger and held at a more ideal angle of 45 degrees, confirming growing confidence and self-assurance. The fingers are straighter, reflecting greater ease of self-expression. The three major lines of heart, head, and life are more equally developed, reflecting a resolve to be more harmonious in all aspects of life. The whole hand is clearer, without too many scattered lines obstructing the three major lines. The quadrangle, shaped by the heart and head lines, is more evenly formed, indicating our ability to balance our reason and feeling. In addition, the mount of Venus, which relates to our body, vitality, and enthusiasm, is usually better developed in length, width, and height, reflecting a desire to live a fuller life.

ERIC: A CASE OF A DOMINANT RIGHT HAND

Eric is right-handed. We can see the contrast between his hands. Eric's right hand has a beautifully formed quadrangle in comparison with his left hand, where the heart and head lines are joined to form a single line. The balanced quadrangle reveals Eric's great determination to think and act in a more harmonious manner than he has in the past. The fused lines of the inactive hand, however, show that Eric needs to guard against subjectivity and indiscriminate enthusiasm. Otherwise, he may fall back into old behavior patterns when exposed to challenging situations.

Eric

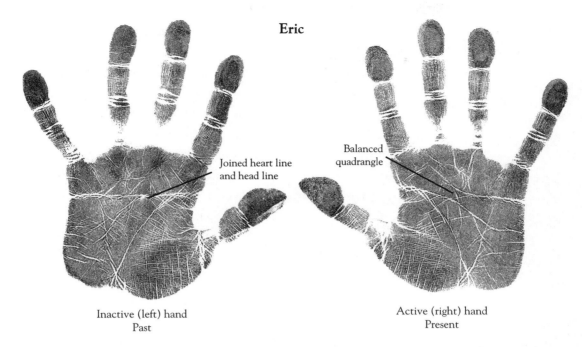

Joined heart line and head line

Balanced quadrangle

Inactive (left) hand
Past

Active (right) hand
Present

A comparative study of Eric's two hands reveals how thoughts and habits from the past form the template that determines present behavior. Eric's resolve to change for the better can be seen in his active hand. Note the development of the heart line in the active (in this case, right) hand compared to the inactive hand.

Nathan

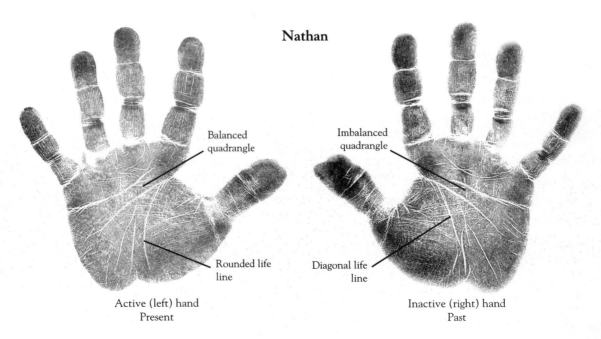

Balanced quadrangle

Rounded life line

Imbalanced quadrangle

Diagonal life line

Active (left) hand
Present

Inactive (right) hand
Past

A study of Nathan's hands reveals that an evolution has taken place from his inactive to his active hand, as shown by the improved formation of major lines.

NATHAN: WHEN THE LEFT HAND IS DOMINANT

Since Nathan writes with his left hand, we consider this to be his active hand. Occasionally, we meet someone who uses the less progressive hand to write with; in this case we need to examine the lines and signs on both hands to determine which one is dominant.

In Nathan's left hand, the three major lines are more balanced than in his right hand. The heart line is equal in length to the head line, creating a balanced quadrangle. We can compare these features to the uneven development of the heart and head lines in the inactive right hand. The life line in the left hand is also rounder than the diagonally formed life line in the right. The diagonal life line shows that Nathan has a tendency to make life difficult for himself. He often finds himself in problematic situations in which he feels that he is swimming against the current. The rounded life line in the left hand reflects his resolve to be attuned to the dynamic of each situation so that he acts appropriately. He has the desire to be more flexible and, therefore, less tense.

Although these signs indicate that Nathan has made a commitment to feel more at ease with himself and others than he has in the past, the negative right-hand tendencies are still part of his makeup. Nathan needs to guard against impulsive, rigid behavior—his legacy from the past.

The Role of Karma

In *The Divine Romance*, Paramahansa Yogananda explains the law of cause and effect:

You are born with about seventy-five percent of your life predetermined by your past. You will make up the remaining twenty-five percent. If you yourself, through your own free choice and effort of will, do not determine what that twenty-five percent will be, the seventy-five percent will make the twenty-five percent for you, and you will become a puppet. That is, you will be ruled absolutely by your past, by the influence and effects of your past tendencies.*

In Sanskrit the concept of cause and effect is known as karma. According to Vedic philosophy there are three different forms of karma directly relating to our inactive and active hands. The first karma, *sanchit*, refers to all the deeds we have done in all our former lives up to the present birth. *Sanchit* constitutes a mixture of all the positive and negative karma we have created and it is found in our inactive hand. As it is almost impossible to experience all the effects of our past in one lifetime, we enter into this life with just a portion of our karmic bank account. This portion is referred to as *prarabdh* and it is found in the active hand. *Kriyaman* is the karma that relates to our free will. The actions we eventually take, based on our freedom of choice, have a direct effect on our present and past, as seen in our active and inactive hands. *Kriyaman* is the unknown factor. It is the power of our will and discrimination to move forward

*Paramahansa Yogananda, *The Divine Romance* (Los Angeles: Self-Realization Fellowship, 1986), 304.

or backward. Used positively, *kriyaman* is our ability to exercise free will in order to realize our desires and accomplish all the resolutions of our active hand. Used negatively, *kriyaman* is our inability to make conscious positive choices; we fall back into bad habits of the past, consequently creating deeper karmic debts.

When we exercise the power of discriminating intelligence (*buddhi*) we make appropriate choices. When we are overwhelmed by the desire for sensory gratification (*manas*) at the expense of reason, we can make unwise decisions.

The Significance of the Inactive Hand in Our Relationships

Whether we use our *kriyaman* karma, our 25 percent, to transcend old patterns and create new inroads of positive behavior is dependent upon the environment in which we find ourselves. It may be able to support our positive intentions or it may cause us to slip back into old behavior patterns.

Checking both hands, then, becomes especially important in the instance of long-term partnerships, such as marriage or work relationships, as these are the foundation of our environment. The active hand shows how an individual projects outwardly, but the inactive hand shows inherited traits and characteristics. Individuals contemplating marriage may be attracted to one another on the basis of their active hands alone. But it is prudent to be aware of inactive-hand tendencies, which may seem to be lying dormant but may be activated by

unexpected circumstances. Feeling that another is in harmony with our positive resolutions, we may depend on our partner's encouragement to become the best we can be. Unaware of our partner's own subconsciously raging battle, on a day-to-day level we may find that he or she has little energy left to support us. In fact, our partner's negativity may cause our own negativity to appear. On a positive note, this type of relationship may act as a mirror, enabling us to confront areas in ourselves that otherwise, in a less intimate setting, we might not have been aware of. Both must be willing, however, to support each other's growth and not fall into the patterns of negative behavior.

MARIO AND AUDREY

Mario has a beautifully balanced quadrangle in his active hand, which in this case is his left hand. A shorter heart line in his inactive hand, however, indicates a subconscious tendency to rationalize situations at the expense of feelings. Audrey also has a balanced quadrangle in her active (right) hand and a shorter heart line in her inactive one. When they first met, Audrey was Mario's language instructor in a local college. Audrey and Mario were attracted to each other almost from the first, drawn by each other's open, generous spirit. Mario was impressed by Audrey's caring, sensitive manner with her students, and she found him to be receptive and considerate. Their relationship soon blossomed into a romance and, in time, they married. They thought they understood each other well, but in fact, their relationship had not been tested

Two Complementary Souls

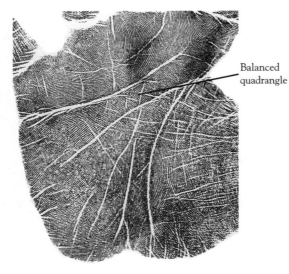

Balanced
quadrangle

Mario's active hand

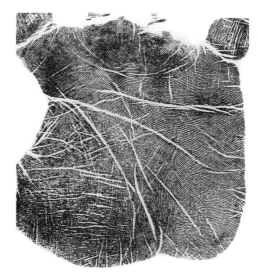

Mario's inactive hand

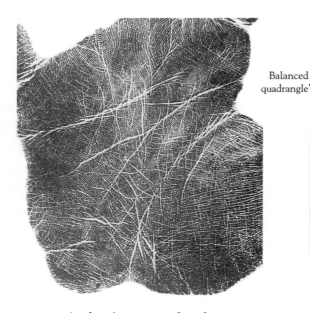

Audrey's inactive hand

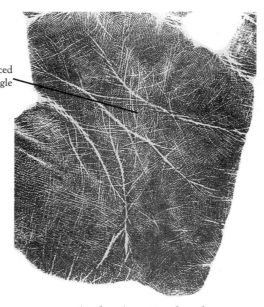

Balanced
quadrangle

Audrey's active hand

*Note the balanced quadrangle in Mario's active left hand (heart and head lines equal
in length). Note the balanced quadrangle in Audrey's active right hand.*

by the intimacy of living together day to day.

On one occasion, Mario made elaborate preparations for a romantic weekend getaway. Audrey, who had given her class a pop quiz and had papers to mark, phoned Mario at the last minute to cancel their plans. Although she recognized that Mario would be disappointed, she counted on his considerate nature to be flexible, suggesting that they reschedule to another weekend. Mario was extremely hurt. He had counted on Audrey giving top priority to their relationship and felt betrayed by her seemingly nonchalant attitude toward his romantic weekend. Each had expectations of the other based upon qualities reflected in the long heart lines of their active hands.

Audrey was angry with Mario for not understanding her need to fulfill the obligations of her work. Mario was angry with Audrey for not recognizing how much this weekend meant to him. They did not speak to each other for several days. Under pressure, each fell into patterns inherited from their pasts, reflected in the short heart lines of their inactive hands.

Finally, with the help of a trusted friend, they came to understand the new dynamic in their relationship. It was not unreasonable for Mario to have expected Audrey to plan her work schedule so that it would not conflict with the weekend; nor was it unreasonable for Audrey to rely on Mario to accommodate her last-minute demands. It was, however, unloving for Mario to judge Audrey for being inconsiderate, and for Audrey to judge Mario for being inflexible. Their anger stemmed from thwarted

expectations. Even though their conscious desire is to be loving regardless of the circumstances, as shown by the long heart lines in their active hands, Audrey and Mario are having to work hard to make their intention a reality as they lack the support of strong subconscious heart lines.

AIDAN: PROGRESS BEING MADE

Aidan has an overdeveloped Mars negative in his inactive hand (denoting an explosive temper). We find a more balanced Mars negative in his active hand, telling us that Aidan has made a resolution to control his emotional outbursts.

We would not recommend that Aidan work in an irritating environment or marry someone who may provoke his potentially volatile temper. Aidan needs a peaceful environment in which he will have the time to develop his resolve to be even tempered.

CREATIVE TENSION: THE DYNAMICS OF CHANGE

Not only do the differences between the inactive hand and the active hand represent our resolve to change our past negative tendencies, but the differences themselves can create the impulse to evolve from one behavior pattern to another.

Marlene's heart line is equally long in both hands. She does not feel the need to become more warmhearted and outgoing because she naturally demonstrates these characteristics. Her

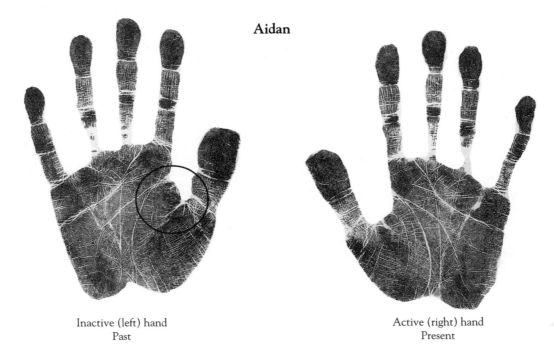

Aidan

Inactive (left) hand
Past

Active (right) hand
Present

Note the overdeveloped Mars negative in Aidan's inactive hand.

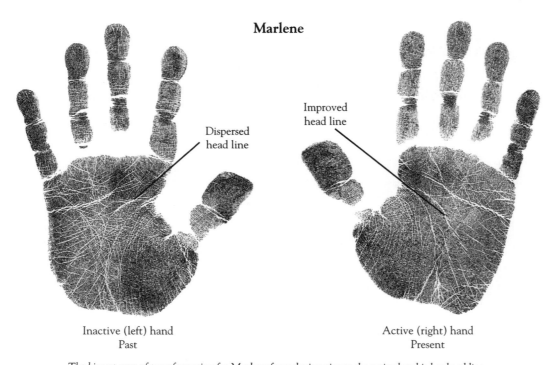

Marlene

Dispersed
head line

Improved
head line

Inactive (left) hand
Past

Active (right) hand
Present

The biggest area of transformation for Marlene from the inactive to the active hand is her head line.

head line, however, is quite different in both hands. In her inactive hand, it is dispersed, indicating confusion and a lack of focus. In her active hand, her head line is more defined, an indication of a much greater degree of organization and direction. She wants to write a cookbook, but each time she starts she becomes sidetracked by her willingness to help her family with their projects. In this case, the generosity of spirit shown in her strong heart line is not being guided and sustained by an equally long head line in both hands. The significant discrepancy in the formation of the head line between Marlene's inactive and active hands points to the area she feels most compelled to transform. The pain she feels each time she fails to achieve her goal may either cause her to relinquish her dream or inspire her to accomplish her objective.

When there is a disparity between the features of one hand and the other, an imbalance is created. The discomfort and friction produced by this state of imbalance can be equated with a feeling of "divine discontent," which consequently motivates us to evolve.

For instance, an infant tries to follow his father up the stairs, but his legs are not long enough to climb them. The contrast between the physique of the father and son is much like the differing strengths of the lines seen in our two hands. The infant is inspired to imitate his father's example and, in time, will develop the strength and coordination to do so.

The impulse to change seen in a stronger line in the active hand will also, in time, propel the weaker one in the inactive hand to become similar in length and strength. Therefore, wherever a discrepancy is found between the two hands, this will be the area of greatest friction and the cutting edge of personal transformation.

With effort come the rewards. By rebalancing the two hands, the corresponding brain hemispheres are also simultaneously stimulated. When we are able to harmonize the conscious (active) with the subconscious (inactive), we come to terms with the reality of who we are, where we have been, and what we are in the process of becoming.

When a particular feature of both hands is the same, we do not experience the feeling of "divine discontent" that could motivate us to evolve. For example, we may have difficulty being sensitive to the feelings of others when our heart lines are short in both hands. Thus, we may not question how our behavior affects those around us, and we are unlikely to change how we respond emotionally. A longer head line in the active hand, however, indicates that we are motivated to think differently.

Sweeping Changes

The active hand reflects what we are struggling to become. The inactive shows where we have been. A large discrepancy between the lines and signs of the inactive and active hands can be an indication of a real challenge. We may have the desire to make sweeping changes in our life as shown in the active hand, but signs in the inactive hand may suggest that such resolutions will be difficult to implement.

Perhaps in the interim between lives, the realization dawns on us that previous lives have not been used to their best advantage. We may decide to make amends, to "catch up" and improve our karma. But in our enthusiasm, we may create a gap between who we are fundamentally, as shown by the inactive hand, and high expectations that are inadequately supported, as shown by the active hand. What may follow is a level of stress so high that it overwhelms us at a very deep level. We may have one existential crisis after another as we are buffeted about between our past and present selves. Yet when we find such differences between our hands, we have great potential to move quickly in our evolution. We need only to remain centered and not give in to feeling helpless or overwhelmed.

Friction and discomfort are a normal part of the growth process. These feelings remind us that we are still on track and maintaining our resolve, and they act as a catalyst for continued change.

Few Changes

From a comparative analysis of our two palms, identifiable differences indicate that for better or worse, personal transformation is taking place in our life. For example, if there is a short heart line in the inactive hand and a longer one in the active hand, we want to become more loving and will consciously work toward this goal. Change can also come in the form of regression, whereby patterns become more imbalanced from the inactive to the active hand.

Although it is very rare, a marked overall similarity in the lines and signs of both hands suggests that we are on vacation. This can represent one of two cases. In the first case, we are unaware of the need to change and consequently lack the motivation to grow. For example, if we find wavy head lines in both hands, we may be uncertain. As this line is the same in both hands, we may be unaware of the need to become more decisive. There is no motivating factor that propels us to think differently. A wavy head line in our inactive hand and a straighter line in our active hand shows that we can become more reliable, but it may be a challenge to accomplish this resolve.

In the second case of similar patterns in both hands, we have realized a certain resolve that we have been working toward and now feel satisfied in this respect. For example, we may not need to change if we have already developed a loving heart as indicated by a long heart line originating from the mount of Jupiter in both hands.

MAURICE: A CASE OF REGRESSION

Maurice's case is more complex than those we have studied so far. After a quick glance at the right and left hands we might assume the right hand is the active one. It has a more rounded Venus mount below the thumb, with a longer life line encircling it; a longer head line free from any interruptions (note the islanded head line in the left hand); a heart line reaching up to the mount of Jupiter, below the index finger (whereas in the left hand it curves down toward

Maurice

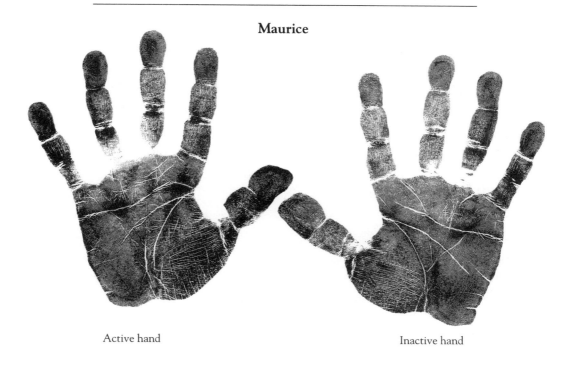

Active hand

Inactive hand

A quick look at Maurice's hands would lead one to think he is right-handed, owing to the better line formation in his right hand. But this is one of those rare cases in which the person was using his less progressive hand at the time this handprint was taken.

the head line, obstructing the "landing strip of the angels"); and a stronger thumb with a more dynamic phalanx of will. All of these are positive indications. Maurice, however, uses his left hand as his dominant hand, making his right hand the inactive one.

This phenomenon is explained in Vedic palmistry texts. Maurice, upon entering the astral realm, was able to review his past. He formulated new resolutions as to how he would like to express himself, given another opportunity. Just as he was about to incarnate, however, he got "cold feet." Instead of going forward with all his positive resolutions, Maurice hesitated

and decided to hold onto what was more familiar and secure.

With time, however, Maurice began to feel confined. He felt that he was capable of accomplishing much more. Maurice started exercising his more progressive (inactive) hand by using it to keep a daily journal. This engaged the opposite brain hemisphere. He wrote for at least fifteen minutes each night before going to sleep and within six months was able to see positive results.

According to Vedic literature, if the hemisphere that contains the hidden treasure of positive resolutions is activated by using its corresponding (opposite) hand, we may be able to break the confines that prevent us from living out the resolutions that we have already formulated. People who write with their less-developed hand are often sensitive and somewhat ambidextrous.

Fortunately, Maurice was a pianist whose hands were already very strongly developed. Therefore, it wasn't too difficult for him to try writing with his right hand. Over time, he found himself reacting to situations differently and attracting many opportunities that previously he would have resisted. The change in hands actually brought about an improvement in his career as well, culminating in successful musical recordings. Maurice switched to being right-handed. Such cases are rare, and it is not advisable to suggest changing hands without an in-depth comparative study of both hands.

NED: A CASE OF AMBIDEXTERITY

The truly ambidextrous person can use both hands with equal ease, even for fine motor tasks such as writing. While this might appear to be an advantage, in fact it suggests that we may be unable to focus on developing distinct aspects of our nature. Neither hand is inactive but neither is dominant. We may find that our energies are dispersed, leaving us confused and uncertain.

If the hands indicate extreme talent, we may benefit from such diversification. But

Ned

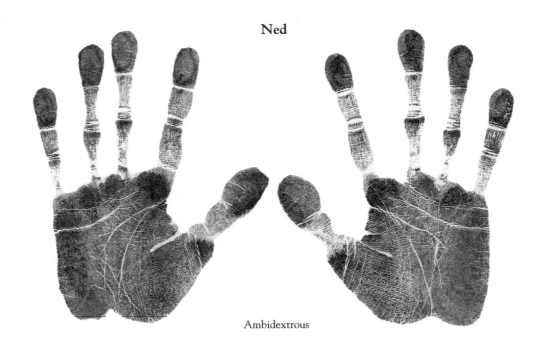

Ambidextrous

Although Ned uses both hands interchangeably, he prefers to write with his left hand. In terms of evolution, however, it is his right hand that shows progression. Note the greater stability in the Venus and Luna mounts, the longer heart line and life line, and the more balanced quadrangle.

more likely, our ambidexterity may create ambiguity and uncertainty in our nature. We may have mixed feelings regarding others—perhaps as an extension of our own ambivalence. At times we may find it difficult to be decisive, focused, and calm about important matters in life. Coordination, precision, accurate judgment, and firmness of opinion need to be developed. Because of our vacillation, we may find it difficult to express ourselves freely. If we can overcome our hesitancy, we can move toward a more determined and dynamic state of mind.

Often, what at first may seem to be a case of ambidexterity is not really so; in most instances, one hand is usually dominant. In addition to noting which is our preferred hand for writing, we can take note of which side we tend to sleep on, which foot goes first when walking, which eye is more sensitive (for example, which eye tears first flow from), and which hand we extend to retrieve a falling object. If more positive evolution is also found in the lines and signs of the hand believed to be the dominant hand, then we could concentrate on strengthening that hand by using it for fine motor tasks.

MONITORING OUR PROGRESS

Not only can we see progress taking place from our inactive to our active hand, but we can also monitor the changes continually taking place in our lives. These changes can be a direct result of shifts in our environment, or they may come as a result of our own changing priorities, attitudes, and perceptions toward our environment. If we are given a promotion at work, for instance, our feeling of achievement might be confirmed by the appearance of a strong Sun line, the line of success. Or the same promotion could bring feelings of anxiety, resulting in the Sun line fading. Although we may not always be in a position to choose the circumstances in which we find ourselves, we do have a choice with regard to how we will react to them. These changes are registered in our hands.

AUDREY:
A CASE OF EVOLUTIONARY PROGRESS

The progressive pattern of Audrey's heart line in the active right hand shows her desire to be more compassionate. Her inactive heart line reflects the difficulty she has expressing her emotions, in spite of the extended heart line in her active hand. It is one thing to want to be more generous with our feelings; without the constant practice of substituting positive new habits for the old, we can easily be drawn back into negative patterns of behavior.

Handprints taken at regular intervals will confirm the progress we are making. If the heart line in the active hand shrinks and begins to resemble the heart line of the inactive hand, then we are lacking either the supportive environment or the willpower to break new ground. If the inactive heart line grows to match the longer heart line of the active hand, then the desire to change is becoming a reality.

Audrey

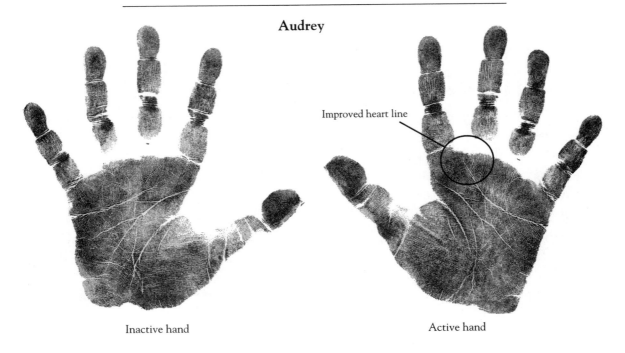

Inactive hand   Active hand

*The progressive pattern of Audrey's heart line in the active right hand
shows her desire to be more compassionate.*

The Significance of Changing Lines on the Inactive Hand

Changes are most likely to occur on the active hand, since this is the hand that most directly reflects tendencies in our current life. Changes that can be detected on the inactive hand—even minute ones—are even more dramatic because they mean our very foundation is being reworked.

LILLIAN: A CASE OF CHANGING LINES ON THE INACTIVE HAND

Sometimes greater changes occur on the inactive hand than on the active hand. In Lillian's case, just three months after her first handprints were taken, profound changes were evident on her inactive hand. According to Vedic palmistry, our inactive hand is like the root system of a plant, while the active hand can be compared to the flower, which is immediately observable. The roots reflect the patterns of our last three lives. The flower represents the karmic resolutions we have made. When the inactive hand changes, our very roots are shifting.

Can We Rewrite the Past?

If our inactive hand reflects our past, can we alter our past by changing the lines and signs in our inactive hand? Can our history be rewritten? Is it possible to undo what has been done? Let's take another look at Audrey's handprints.

The short heart line on her inactive hand

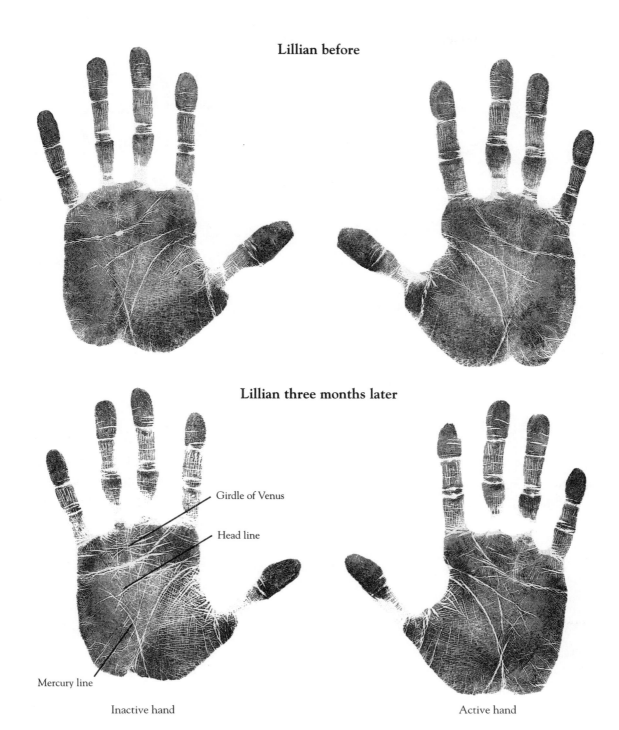

Lillian before

Lillian three months later

Girdle of Venus

Head line

Mercury line

Inactive hand

Active hand

Notice the changes that occurred in Lillian's hands over the course of three months.
While her active hand did not change as significantly, her inactive hand reveals the development
of a girdle of Venus and a longer head line and Mercury line.

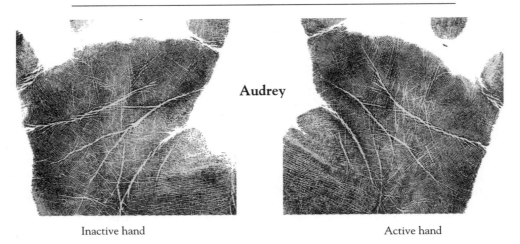

Inactive hand   Active hand

Repeated handprints will indicate whether the inactive hand's heart line grows or the active heart line shrinks.
If Audrey maintains her positive resolve to be more loving, her inactive heart line will grow to reflect the resolutions shown
by the longer heart line of the active hand.

is the result of unfeeling behavior in the past. At some point, however, either at the end of her last life or in the astral interim between lives, she felt remorse and resolved to be more loving in the future. This desire is reflected in a longer heart line in her active hand. But Audrey's emotional bank account is pretty much in the red. Even with good intentions, she continues to attract, by the effects of her actions in past lives, people who might not behave nicely toward her. Whether the new Audrey pays off old debts or incurs further debts depends on how she reacts to others' negative behavior toward her. If she fails to recognize her past tendency to be un-loving, she may perceive herself to be victimized. She may respond by disliking people further, causing her active heart line to shrink. In this case, she would be repeating the trends of the past. If, however, she maintains her positive resolve to be more loving in spite of

encountering negative behavior, her inactive heart line will grow to reflect the expectations shown by the longer heart line of the active hand. Her positive resolution to be more generous toward people is no longer a wish but has become a reality. According to Vedic palmistry, her karmic emotional debts will have been paid.

Does this mean that Audrey can erase her past insensitivity to people by growing a longer heart line in her inactive hand? We think of events in history as linear—that is, finite points in time and space. In Vedic palmistry, however, time and space are of no significance, since the prime concern is the soul, which is infinite. Features of our inactive hand that reflect negative behavior patterns simply show us the extent to which we are out of touch with our soul nature. The study of palmistry is concerned with whether the mind separates from consciousness by identifying with an event, or whether, as shown by yogis in the highest state of awareness, known as *samadhi*, we can live in the moment (event) yet stay connected with consciousness.

The presence of the heart line could be compared to a light bulb. If the switch is not turned on, we will not see the light. This does not mean there is no electricity. If Audrey's short heart line reflects her unawareness of loving, it does not mean that love does not exist. As soon as she becomes sensitive to others, the switch is turned on, allowing love to flow. Now she might have to pay back the debt of unkindness to those people she has hurt; but if she can do this, she will have realized her astral commitments.

Timings on the Major Lines and Destiny Line

Timings are used to pinpoint both positive and challenging chronological periods that may occur during our lives (see the illustration on timings above). Although timings can be done on each line of the hand, for the purpose of this book, only timings on the major lines and the destiny line will be illustrated.

Find point A (where the Jupiter finger meets the palm) and point B (where the thumb meets the palm). Draw an arc (AB) between points A and B and bisect it at point C. Find point D (where the Mercury finger meets the palm) and extend D down toward point E. DE should be equal to AC. Point E will usually be found where the heart line terminates. Connect CE. This is the base line of the mental mounts. Bisect line CE at F; CF at G; and FE at H. Draw perpen-

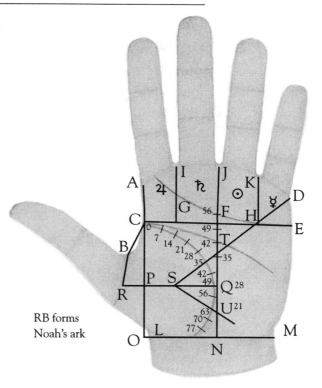

Timings on the lines.

dicular lines GI, FJ, and HK. Points I, J, and K are usually found between the fingers. These lines border the mounts of Jupiter, Saturn, Sun, and Mercury. The time zones CG, GF, FH, and HE cover the years 0–21, 21–42, 42–63, and 63 on, respectively. Each of these sections is further subdivided into three segments of seven years each. The timing of events that relate to the head or heart line can be determined by using the gauge indicated by line CE. Draw a line perpendicular to and through line CE that extends until it intersects the line in question.

Line LM is drawn first by finding point L, located at the base of the mount of Venus where it meets the wrist. This line is drawn parallel to line

CE and terminates at point M, which is located at the base of the mount of Luna. These two mounts, however, may not be equal in length. Therefore, line LM may cut through the base of Luna if this mount is overdeveloped (too long), or a gap may appear between LM and the base of Luna if this mount is underdeveloped (too short).

Next we will locate the center point of the mount of Venus. Find point N by bisecting line LM. Draw line NF perpendicular to LM. Extend line LM under the base of the thumb. Draw line OC perpendicular from this extension of LM. Bisect line OC at point P. Point P is the center of the vertical axis of Venus. Draw line PQ, equal in length and parallel to ON. Extend this line beyond the base of the thumb. Point R is located where this line crosses Noah's Ark, the joint where the thumb meets the mount of Venus. Bisect RQ at S. Point S is the center of the mount of Venus.

Draw diagonal line SD, which intersects line NF at point T. Point U is found on line NF below point Q, so that Q bisects line TU. Draw line SU. Timings on the life line are indicated by the following: ST intersects the life line at age 35; SQ intersects the life line at age 49; and SU intersects the life line at age 63. Draw in nine equal segments on the life line between point C (age 0) to the intersection of line SU (age 63). Each segment represents a seven-year period through the ages of 7, 14, 21, 28, 35, 42, 49, 56, and 63. To continue the timings after age 63, use the same seven-year increments seen in the diagram as 70, 77, and so on.

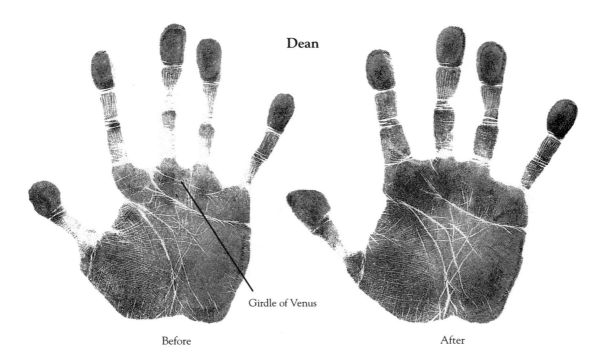

Dean

Girdle of Venus

Before   After

Note the disappearance of the girdle of Venus in the "after" handprint.

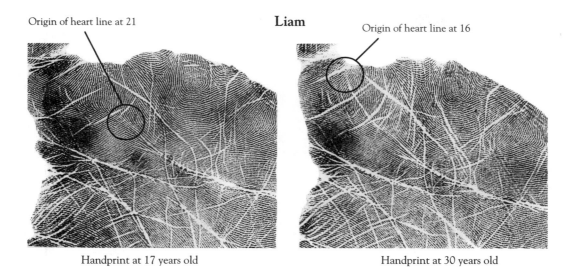

Origin of heart line at 21

Liam

Origin of heart line at 16

Handprint at 17 years old   Handprint at 30 years old

Note the extension of the heart line in the second handprint.

Timings on the destiny line are determined by the same template used for the life line. They are indicated by the following: SU intersects the destiny line at age 21; SQ at age 28; and ST at age 35. Three equal seven-year segments marking the ages of 42, 49, and 56 are drawn on the destiny line between age 35 and where the destiny line intersects the heart line. The location of the destiny line can be found on either side of line NF. Where necessary, extend lines ST, SQ, and SU to intersect with the destiny line.

DEAN: THE LOST GIRDLE OF VENUS

Dean had a beautiful girdle of Venus at the age of twenty-one, indicating a strongly artistic disposition. At the age of twenty-eight, however, the entire girdle has disappeared. Does this mean that Dean was never actually creative?

In Vedic palmistry, the resolution and outcome of a particular pattern of behavior is re-vealed by studying the origin and termination of the lines. In Dean's case, the disappearing girdle of Venus suggests that he did not nurture his talent when he was twenty-one. His priorities changed. He opened up a dry-cleaning business and stopped painting.

LIAM: A MEMORY FROM THE PAST

A change in the length, and especially the origin, of a line shows an altered awareness of consciousness. For example, when Liam was seventeen, his grandmother, who lived with the family, passed away. His heart line at that time originated at the age of twenty-one. Although such an event normally evokes strong emotions, Liam found the experience neither particularly memorable nor even especially moving.

Four years later, at the age of twenty-one, Liam became more connected with the emotional side of his nature. As the years passed, his maturity and sensitivity developed. In time, the actual origin of the heart line changed, reflecting his deeper level of emotional involvement with life. Handprints taken in his early thirties show the heart line originating at age sixteen.

When Liam looks back over the years, he is suddenly flooded with memories of his grandmother when he was seventeen. He has come to feel the full impact of her passing, although he was not able to identify with it at the time.

The development of the lines and signs on our hands is a result of both our positive and negative thought processes. The markings indicate the type of circumstances we are likely to attract and the behavior we are most likely to display. Lines and signs that correlate chronologically with events in our life determine not only the nature of these events, but to what degree we are aware of our thoughts, feelings, and behavior as we experience them. Are we

hurtful, sarcastic, and uncaring or helpful and loving? Do we objectively perceive the nature of the circumstances we attract while maintaining an emotional and mental equilibrium within them? In this context, then, our passage through life is simply the means by which we learn to develop consciously our sensitivity and awareness.

In our example, Liam experienced an increased awareness when he turned seventeen. Who we have been and what we become are important evolutionary concerns. Consciousness, however, is the issue, not whether Liam's understanding came at seventeen or seventy. The timings (see figure on page 85) of the origins of the major lines indicate when we become more self-aware. The idea here is not to dwell on the past, either in this life or in past incarnations, but on how conscious we are. After all, we need to live and work in the present. This is where our evolution takes place.

Jude

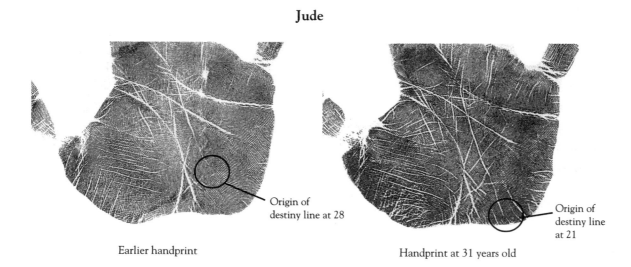

Origin of destiny line at 28

Earlier handprint

Origin of destiny line at 21

Handprint at 31 years old

Notice the change in the origin of Jude's destiny line.

An awareness of the cycles of life can broaden our perspective on the purpose of existence, however. History repeats itself. With an understanding of our patterns and cycles, we can decide which habits contribute to our happiness and which detract from it.

JUDE: A CHANGE IN DESTINY

When Jude was twenty-one, he would go fishing with his grandfather, a retired chef. At the time, Jude had no idea what he wanted to do with his life. Sometimes, he and his grandfather talked about Jude opening a restaurant, but Jude never took the suggestion seriously. For the next seven years, he was a jack-of-all-trades. But when, at the age of twenty-eight, he suddenly had the opportunity to become a chef, he took it and worked in a restaurant kitchen for three years. He discovered he had a real talent for cooking. At the age of thirty-one, Jude opened his own restaurant.

A print taken at the age of thirty-one shows that his destiny line begins at the age of twenty-one, not twenty-eight as before. Now, Jude realizes that the idea of becoming a restaurateur was planted in his mind by his grandfather many years earlier, when Jude was twenty-one.

Perhaps when he was twenty-eight, Jude would have attributed his decision to become a chef to simply a random opportunity. It does not mean the fishing trip never happened—it was just filed away and forgotten. But three years later, at the age of thirty-one, he can acknowledge the true significance of his grandfather's influence. Once the event is remembered, it registers consciously as a line.

THE ART OF PREDICTION

The lines of the hand can give us information about our present tendencies, past patterns of behavior, and intentions for the future. Hence, we can determine how successfully we are using our potential for making our goals a reality.

Winning the lottery early in life is no guarantee of financial security. If we use up the principal and fail to make wise investments, we can lose everything we have gained. We may have a strong destiny line, but if we do not nurture it, we may not find it there in the future.

How Does Knowledge of the Past Affect the Future?

Who we are tomorrow is an extension of what we are today. We are today what we

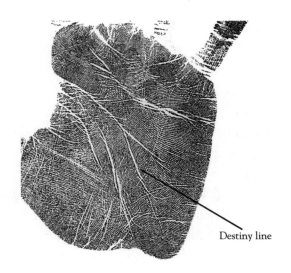

Destiny line

Note that the destiny line is terminating at the head line. With awareness, this formation can change.

were yesterday. Our present, therefore, is linked both to the future and to the past. If we do not invest our principal—or nurture the positive developments we have made in the past—we risk losing for the future all that we have gained from the past.

Mozart showed great talent for music at the young age of four. In his previous life, he must have established very strong roots in his destiny line so that in this life, it did not take long to reconnect with his musical talent.

In palmistry, we stress the importance of connecting with the past. We need to be aware of former habits that have resulted in our present circumstance. By the same logic, then, the present patterns suggest future behavior. Habits are not easily broken, but past trends can be changed. We can learn how to strengthen those tendencies that we wish to develop and how to break those habits that are detrimental to our success.

Too often people look to the future or dwell in the past and forget all about living in the present. To return to our financial analogy, it is in the present that we either invest the principal to accumulate interest or squander it so that we end up penniless. Lines register on the inactive hand if our awareness remains on a subconscious level. If our lines are equally apparent in both hands, we are conscious of our roots. Lines present in the active hand and not in the inactive one indicate that we are creating new patterns in our current lifetime through conscious determination and motivation.

The origin of a line tells us the cause of a particular trend. The termination of a line is the effect. Therefore, it is our awareness of a trend's cause and effect that gives us the power to alter a line. Once we become conscious of how we became who we are, the lines on our hands reflect the expansion of our consciousness. The point of origin of a line changes because we ourselves possess greater insight into the past. This in turn may alter how we think about the future, and therefore the termination of a line might change, too. As we reassess past and future, the lines on our hands respond.

It is important to guard against making predictions, as we may become preoccupied by worries and fears for the future, distracting us from focusing on the present. But past trends can reveal what is likely to happen in the future. A destiny line abruptly terminating at the head line could reliably "predict" that faulty thinking is a problem, which could cause us to lose a job in the future. If we are aware of this potentially destructive trait, however, we could change our thinking to avert a misfortune. This would be reflected in the hand as the destiny line elongates to extend past our mended head line.

Evolution is often seen as a linear progression from the past to the present and on into the future. If we can begin to think of evolution more in terms of being fully aware in the present, then, like a ripple, our expanded consciousness will affect both our past and our future.

The Importance of Confirming Events in the Active and Inactive Hands

The inactive hand acts like a shadow of the active hand. It is important to check both hands for indications of important events or characteristics.

Let's take the example of Maurice (see pages 78–80) who switched from using his left hand to using his right hand as his active hand. At the age of thirty-eight, Maurice experienced a dramatic seizure. He felt the effects as a loss of sensation. He went for CAT scans and saw many specialists who could only speculate as to what had happened, since there was no physical evidence of anything wrong. At thirty-eight years of age in Maurice's active hand we find a long, clear head line. At thirty-eight in the inactive hand, however, we find an island in the head line, which reflects a blockage.

If Maurice's dominant hand had been his left hand, he would have experienced the effects of the island more seriously and there is the likelihood that this would have been confirmed by the doctor's findings. But because he was right-handed, he felt more the phantom effects of the island than the real thing. All findings of the active hand must be confirmed in the inactive hand.

For example, we may have a Sun line in the inactive hand that is not present in the active one. Talent is there in latent form; however, we have to be consciously aware of the potential we sense on an intuitive level. This capability must now be brought to awareness in the active hand. If the Sun line is present in the active hand alone, we are working on developing this talent in the present life; it is a new experience and must be nurtured.

Maurice

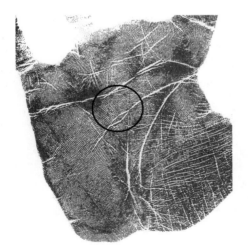 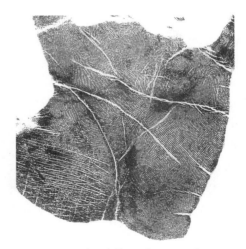

Inactive hand (formerly active)   Active hand (formerly inactive)

Note the island on Maurice's head line in his inactive left hand.

Conclusion

YOUR IDEAL HANDS—
A VISUALIZATION TECHNIQUE

Each of us is unique, as shown by the distinct patterns in the lines and signs of our hands. The hands reflect our individuality and our personal journey through life. Finding the balance as we experience life, however, is our greatest challenge. In our personal quest to achieve equilibrium, we are influenced by the unrelenting, universal forces of attraction and repulsion. We therefore need a structure to help guide us through these extremes.

In nature there are cycles and patterns that reflect balance. At dusk and dawn, for example, light and dark merge. Polarity or duality, the principle of opposites, ceases to exist at these times; nature displays neutrality or harmony within the greater universal flux of polarity. The example of dusk and dawn suggests that we, as part of nature, can also exhibit the quality of neutrality or balance. We simply need to recognize and implement a pattern that reflects this equilibrium within the human context.

In esoteric palmistry, the concept of ideal hands is the pattern or template that represents balance. It is a composite of the best lines and signs from both hands that indicates equilibrium and points to the mental, physical, and spiritual qualities that each of us ultimately strives to achieve. Developing the characteristics indicated by the ideal hands reflects our increased attunement to the infinite possibilities of spirit—and how we can imagine the best of ourselves to be. For example, there may be positive qualities in our inactive subconscious hand, such as a star on Sun, indicating self-assurance and success, that we would like to see realized in our conscious active hand. There may be negative patterns of thinking and behaving reflected in our active hand that we would like to see disappear—for instance, a ring of Saturn, denoting negative thinking and pessimism. Or we may see few wisdom markings on the mounts of either hand, such as vertical lines, tridents, or flags. We would like to see these markings present on both our conscious and subconscious hands, indicating that we are consciously aware of and working with the talents inherent within us. By taking the best of our past and present and connecting it with our vision of positive resolves for future growth, we can create a template of how we would ideally envision ourselves.

The Visualization of Your Ideal Hands

The concept of creating our ideal hands is a technique of visualization. It is an exercise designed to help us develop positive qualities and eliminate negative ones.

We all have undesirable tendencies; they show up as lines and markings on our hands that indicate inappropriate or nonproductive patterns of thinking. The practice of visualizing our ideal handprints is designed to help break these patterns by introducing a blueprint of new and helpful patterns that, when focused upon, promote equilibrium in our thinking and subsequent behavior.

For example, growing or shortening our fingers may seem a fairly hopeless proposition. But by visualizing a balanced third hand with fingers of an ideal length, we get in touch with those qualities that we see in our ideal fingers. We create fresh patterns of thinking and connect to all the qualities we most wish to nurture in ourselves.

In the following example, Billy is left-handed. We can see well-developed heart and head lines in his active left hand as well as a rounded life line. In his inactive right hand we see that Billy has a shorter heart line pulled to the head line as well as a diagonally placed life line. His head line is well placed, resembling the head line of his active hand. For an ideal template, Billy will imagine the shorter heart line of his inactive subconscious hand growing to reflect the rich resolve of his active heart line, which is better balanced with his head line.

Billy wants very much to be harmonious in his life, which is reflected by the rounded life line in his active hand. However, he can fall into old habits of embracing negative situations—being contrary, resisting what is good for him, and turning away the company of supportive friends. This pattern is shown by the diagonal life line in his inactive hand, which reflects his patterns of behavior in the past. To discourage himself from reverting to these old ways and to encourage the positive resolve of his active hand, he can visualize a rounded life line superimposed over the diagonal life line in his inactive hand.

We can see that Billy also has underdeveloped Mars negative and Luna mounts. The mounts act as the foundation of the hand, so by

Billy

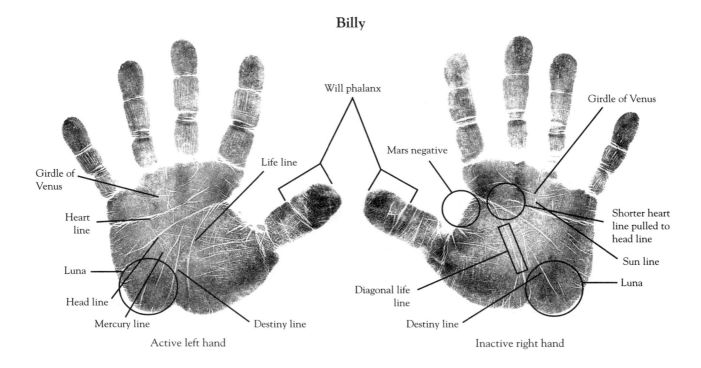

Will phalanx

Girdle of Venus
Heart line
Luna
Head line
Mercury line
Life line
Destiny line

Mars negative
Diagonal life line
Destiny line

Girdle of Venus
Shorter heart line pulled to head line
Sun line
Luna

Active left hand

Inactive right hand

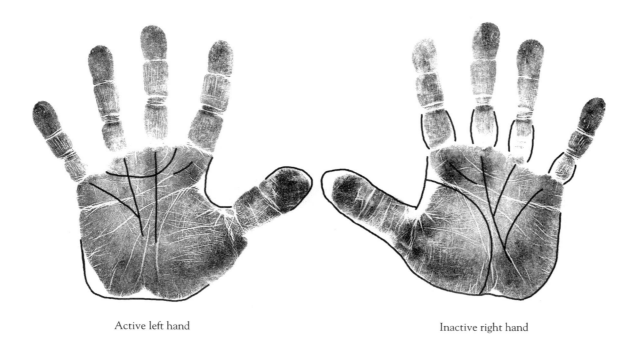

Active left hand

Inactive right hand

The black lines superimposed on the lower pair of handprints show how Billy might compensate for deficits by visualizing his ideal hands.

visualizing better-developed mounts, Billy will be able to tap into the physical energy of Mars negative and the confidence of Luna.

Although he has clearly developed the major lines of heart, head, and life, he has difficulty expressing the rich subconscious abilities, as evidenced by the weaker development of his minor lines. By visualizing stronger minor lines—destiny, Sun, and Mercury—Billy can learn how to make his talents manifest in a more effective way. In addition, we can see that Billy has great artistic sensitivity, as indicated by the presence of a girdle of Venus on his inactive hand. However, this line is not present on his active hand, which suggests that he needs to develop greater emotional stamina to withstand criticism and hurt. He must also guard against viewing life mechanically, which inhibits his inherently innate aesthetic appreciation of life.

By visualizing a rounder girdle of Venus equally strong on both hands, Billy will learn how to channel his sensitivity in a creative manner in order to bring joy to others. In time, he will also direct his visualization toward growing stronger physical phalanxes to support his mental initiatives. We can also see that Billy has a longer logic phalanx than will phalanx in the thumbs of both hands. Visualizing a more developed will phalanx in both hands can enable him to put his thoughts into action.

The image of the ideal hand provides us with an opportunity to free ourselves from the linear constraints of time and space. We can learn to develop our body/mind/soul awareness in this life. We do not have to be trapped in time, laden with negativity, waiting for reincarnations to pass so we can become more evolved. The ideal hand is an alternative path that leads straight to perfection through equilibrium in the present. The only obstacle to our personal growth is ourselves. We can choose to free ourselves from a limited perception of what we can and cannot do in our life by visualizing lines superimposed on both our hands, which can help us develop the positive qualities associated with those lines.

A CHECKLIST OF POINTS TO CONSIDER WHEN ENVISIONING YOUR IDEAL HANDS

In order to determine the template for your ideal hands, you may wish to consult this chapter as a reference for a systematic analysis of what to look for in your own hands.

The fundamental elements of the palm—the mounts, the major and minor lines, and the signs of wisdom or obstruction—can be viewed as layers superimposed upon each other. Similar to the Chinese philosophy of duality or opposites represented by the yin/yang symbol, each element of the hand reflects different degrees of yin (underdeveloped) or yang (overdeveloped). The ideal hand should reflect a balance between the two extremes of yin and yang.

The Mounts

As the first layer, the mounts comprise the land or terrain over which the lines travel. It

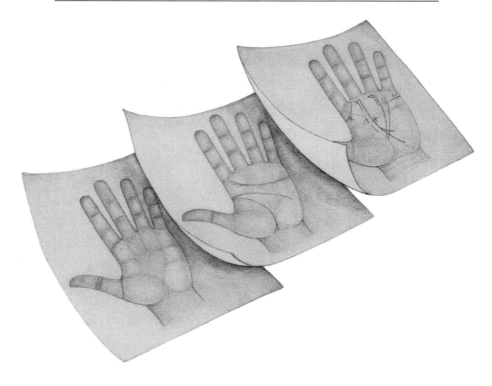

Three levels of consciousness.

is important, therefore, to determine the quality of each underlying mount as well as the interplay between them.

- **Temperature:** In addition to examining the development of each mount—that is, its length, width, and height, which can be underdeveloped or overdeveloped—it is important to check the mount's temperature. Ideally, each mount should be warm, not hot or cold. Too much heat reflects an excess of yang and indicates a need to become more calm and relaxed. In contrast, a cold mount is a sign of excess yin, which reflects an inhibition—perhaps caused by shock or disappointment.

- **Consistency:** Next, check the consistency of each mount. Ideally, each mount, when pressed, should have some resilience or "give" and should be neither too hard nor too soft. Hard mounts reflect an excess of yang—we may be so wound up that we find it difficult to "stop and smell the roses." Soft mounts reveal excess yin and indicate a constitution that is lacking in energy. We can be gentle and kind, but due to our oversensitive and "laid-back" nature, we may procrastinate. Although we are open to receive from others, we have to fight against lethargy and must learn to become more active and expressive in return.

Checking for consistency.

the peaks and troughs that comprise these ridges determines if the texture is coarse—a wide gap; superfine—an extremely narrow gap that can be barely discernible; or medium fine, which indicates balance.

Coarse texture—excess yang—indicates type "A" behavior. We are active and can accomplish a great deal, but in our enthusiasm to forge ahead we may be unaware of the effect that we have on those around us. We need to develop an awareness and sensitivity to the feelings of others.

Superfine texture—excess yin—shows that we are governed primarily by our feeling nature, which at times can overwhelm us. When flooded with emotions, our perception may become clouded and subjective. We need to develop a "tougher skin" and not to take circumstances so seriously.

- **Texture:** Another feature that helps determine the quality of a mount is texture. Texture is created by the papillary ridges that form the top layer of derma, or skin, in the hand. The distance between

- **Color:** The color of the hand also indicates

Coarse texture

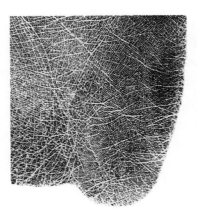

Superfine texture

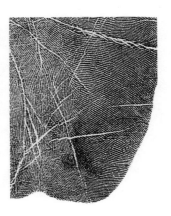

Balanced texture

Texture helps determine the quality of the mounts.

the degree of equilibrium we feel when facing the challenges of life. A red mount indicates too much heat (yang) and shows that we may be too reactive to life events. A white mount that has lost its color (yin) reveals difficulty confronting situations. Pink indicates a nature that can approach situations calmly and "proactively"—one of the habits referred to in Stephen Covey's book *The Seven Habits of Highly Effective People*.*

Signs of Wisdom or Obstruction

Ideally, when the mounts are balanced in width, length, and height, warm to the touch, resilient when pressed, and pink in color, they indicate that a level of objectivity, perception, strength, and sensitivity has been achieved, preparing the groundwork for the development of lines and signs of wisdom.

To the degree that the various features of the mounts are not in harmony, the development of lines and signs of wisdom may be difficult. In these cases, lines of interference and obstruction may be dominant instead. Faulty reasoning, subjectivity, and a poor attitude, perhaps based on thwarted desires and unfulfilled expectations, create friction and discord. If there is no sign of activity on a mount, it is an indication that we have not yet become conscious of the potential

---

*Stephen Covey, *The Seven Habits of Highly Effective People* (New York: Fireside, 1989), 65.

of that area. Remember, the concept of the ideal hand implies that what is excessive (yang) can be minimized and what is missing (yin) can be developed.

- **Signs of wisdom:** Crosses, squares, diamonds, and stars found at the mouth of the quadrangle, where it opens to the mount of Jupiter, as well as the ring of Solomon, which forms an arc on the mount of Jupiter, all reflect a positive expression of this mount. A vertical line on the mount of Saturn—the truth line— is another positive indication of wisdom. A single vertical line or a star on Sun is also a positive sign of success. Three parallel vertical lines on the Mercury mount—the healing stigmata—are an indication of genuine caring for others.

- **Signs of obstruction:** A general rule is that horizontal crossbars or grills indicate static that interferes with the positive expression of a mount. Depending on where the interference is found, we may feel frustrated and unable to realize the potential normally associated with that area of life. Imbalances in temperature, consistency, texture, or color of the mounts also indicate obstructions to progress. Check each mount carefully to determine where the imbalances lie.

- Crosses, stars, or grills on Saturn are negative signs and indicate conflict and tension.

• A cold Moon (Luna mount) needs more heat. We take other people too seriously and need to focus more on our creative impulses. We should think of our emotions, feelings, and sensitivity as powerful tools that we can draw upon to manifest our ideas and thoughts in such diverse areas as making music, preparing delicious food, or creating a beautiful garden. These same tools, however, can become a liability if we remain too yin, or stagnant in our outlook. Remember, it is the mutable nature of our emotions that can equally give rise to noble, creative ideas or to anxiety, fear, and hurt feelings. By integrating the opposite (or yang) expression of the qualities of the Moon, we can learn to eliminate thoughts that undermine our stability. Rather, we use our sensitivity to channel our feelings and impressions in an outward creative flow of energy.

• A hard Venus indicates we need to unwind and relax. Sometimes we might actually find ourselves panting or feeling out of breath. It is great to accomplish a lot, but we need to slow down and take a deep breath.

• If pressure is applied to a Mars positive that has a soft consistency, it will retain an indented shape for a while before returning to its original form. This indicates that we need to develop greater mental endurance, patience, and persistence. We must learn to see tasks or projects that we have started through to final completion. The resulting confidence and sense of fulfillment will encourage us to take on even greater responsibilities.

• An overly red Mars negative with a star shows an excess of yang. We may find ourselves overreacting in our interactions with other people. Instead of mutual agreement and understanding with others, we may create chaos and disharmony. To cool our temper and agitation it would be wise to slowly drink ten glasses of water a day. We should try to avoid stimulating or aggravating environments that can activate our volatile nature. Watch peaceful movies, read inspirational stories, try to eat a balanced diet, and avoid overstimulating food and drink. If we feel our blood beginning to boil, we should count to ten and leave the situation. We will be more objective and in better shape to discuss matters once we have calmed down.

• If Venus is too squeezed, we are letting our shoulders droop. We need to stand erect and breathe deeply from the diaphragm. There is a major artery that passes through the Venus mount. If this area is too tight or is indented, we need to build it up with yoga, deep breathing, country walks, revitalization. We must also learn to express spontaneity of feeling, as inhibiting thoughts may confine the oxygen-rich blood that flows through this artery and through our system, building up the cells and helping to rid the body of toxins. We must visualize a stronger, round, and robust mount of Venus on our ideal hands.

- If our Moon (Luna mount) is shorter than the length of Venus, creating an uneven ground, we can draw a rounder Moon on our ideal hands and visualize it to be strong and steady. Everything begins with our perception, as represented by the Moon. When the Luna mount is too yin, it needs to be developed. Develop your powers of imagination and visualization. Try to see the good. Be positive, be grateful, see the glass half full and not half empty. Do not hold back from challenges—they may be great life lessons, and you will feel sorry at a later date if you did not make the most of them. While checking these points, keep

your own hand in mind. Then draw your hand as you would like it to be. Put the drawing in a place where you will see it when you wake up and go to sleep. Visualize your present hand changing to become your ideal hand.

The Balance of the Major Lines

Each of the three major lines should be equally deep and long and should not be crisscrossed by any interference lines. Check your three lines. Are they equally strong? If not, highlight that area and visualize it becoming stronger. Look at the three cases that follow as good examples.

In the following figure, in the first handprint, you can see that the heart line is overly developed in comparison to the head and life lines. In the middle handprint the head line is more developed than the heart and life lines. In the last handprint it is the life line that is strongest.

- **Dominant heart line:** Are you overly emotional, acting on your feelings without carefully considering the possible results of your actions? For instance, would you indulge the little child's wish for many sweets without realizing that your indulgence might necessitate repeated trips to the dentist? If this is your situation, use a black felt pen and draw a stronger head line on your handprint. Visualize it becoming deeper so that you will not be carried away by emotional impulses without thought for their outcome.

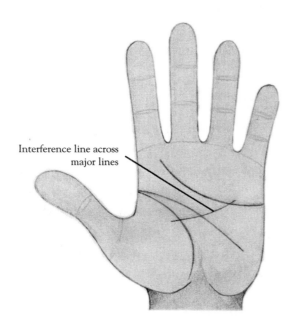

Interference line across major lines

Interference lines across the major lines are considered signs of obstruction.

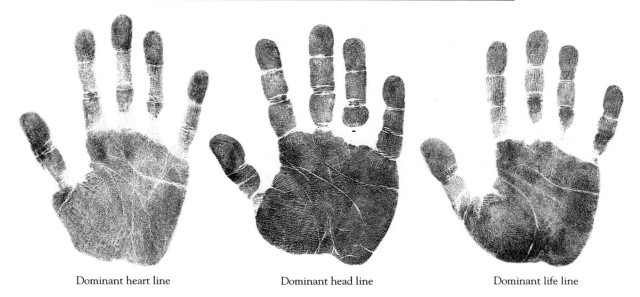

Dominant heart line   Dominant head line   Dominant life line

In the ideal hand the major lines are balanced. Each of these hands has one major line that dominates the others.

• **Dominant head line:** Are you like the second individual, who may keep his feelings in check by overly dominant reason and pragmatism? Learn to trust your feelings more and to express them. Be generous with your heart without worrying what your overly discriminating mind may be cautioning you about. Draw your heart line equal in strength to your head line and visualize it growing deeper and longer. Within a week you will see the difference in your life.

• **Dominant life line:** Lastly, if your life line is strongest and you would like to develop greater heart and head lines, visualize them as equal in strength to the life line. When the life line is strong, yet is unsupported by the other major lines, we may have vitality for life but are unsure and uncommitted

about where we want to direct our energy. Consequently we can get caught up in the tides of time without any deep resolve of heart or mind about why we are expending our energy in dispersed directions.

The Minor Lines

As previously mentioned, three minor lines represent our conscious mind. They show that we are aware of the subconscious richness of our major lines of heart, head, and life and that we have an outlet to express them. Although there are many minor lines, for our purposes we see the lines of destiny, Sun, and Mercury as the most significant.

• **The destiny line:** The presence of the conscious line of destiny reveals that we have a place to pour our heart, a direction to focus our mind upon, and a reason for living—that which inspires our life force to get out of bed each morning. When we have no strong sense of our purpose, we may feel at a loss, akin to a derailed train. The line of destiny can be developed along with the accompanying sense of having a life purpose. If the destiny line stops at the head or heart line, we can visualize it extending past that line, thereby not allowing any faulty reason or subjective emotion to cause us to lose our sense of purpose.

- **The Sun line:** Alongside the destiny line is the Sun line or line of fulfillment. We may have a sense of purpose, as reflected by a strong destiny line, but we may still feel unfulfilled. The presence of a Sun line reveals our committed sense of passion or love for what we are doing and our consequent sense of satisfaction. We are not doing our work mechanically or halfheartedly, dreaming of being somewhere else. We are devoted. We remember the Creator and the fact that it was His love that caused us to be created in the first place. Love is a magnet, and consequently the Sun line attracts all that is good to us. If this line is missing, you can draw it in on your ideal hand and visualize it growing. Become aware of your purpose, your talent, your capability, your reasons for doing things. Are you really developing yourself to the maximum? Become conscious of what you are doing. Developing a sense of love and conscientious care for what you

are doing will bring about the development of the Sun line.

The two minor lines of destiny and Sun, when they are as deep as the major lines of heart, head, and life, reflect a great harmony and integration on all levels of our being—body, mind, and heart. However, we must still fight temptations to be distracted from our purpose or to become attached to the fruits of our actions.

For example, a great star may feel neglected and consequently hurt if his or her fans cheer and applaud someone else. What was originally done out of a sense of fun, inspiration, love, and dedication is now being done with the expectation of reward or acknowledgment. The star was freer before, when there was no expectation, just the joy of performing.

- **The Mercury line:** The presence of the line of Mercury is our assurance that we are not overly attached to the outward fruits of our actions. If we are booed it does not affect us. We keep our sense of humor. We are not looking for outside praise because the work we do is reward enough. For example, when a scientist is totally absorbed in researching a cure for an illness, he or she is not looking to receive a Nobel prize. If the scientist was focused on an outside reward, that person would not be fully in the present and so not fully concentrated. Consequently he or she would be less likely to find the cure—and would not receive the sought-after acknowledgment, either.

The Mercury line, or line of Buddha, is named after the *gautauma* who, searching for the true reliable joy in life, discovered that peace and happiness could be found by going inward. Everything external was finite and impermanent. This line is found on the hands of great storytellers who can use their powers of communication to make us forget ourselves. We sit rapt with attention as they carry us on a trip that makes two hours seem like the blink of an eye!

The Mercury line is the line that transcends time and space. Individuals possessing strong Mercury lines can make us forget that we are hungry or tired, or forget where we are, or forget the fight we just had. They can make things look easy—what may take hours for another person to do they can finish in a flash. Mercury is the line of transcendence—it keeps us from getting bogged down by life and the environment around us. The scientist can work for ten hours solid to come up with his cure. Physical needs, mental preoccupations, emotional upheavals—nothing distracts this individual from focused, joyful self-expression. The line of Mercury ensures that we do not become attached to all the rewards drawn to us by the dedication expressed through our Sun line. For greater freedom of self-expression, visualize this line growing from the life line and reaching beyond the head and heart lines to halfway up the Mercury mount.

Imagine all three minor lines of destiny, Sun, and Mercury to be equally well developed.

Other Suggestions for Visualizing the Ideal Hand

- **Wisdom marks on each mount:** To bring out the best characteristics of your mounts, envision wisdom lines on each of them—a ring of Solomon on Jupiter, a love-of-truth line on Saturn, a star on Sun, and three healing stigmata lines on the mount of Mercury. A well-formed grill on Venus indicates magnetism and a harmonious nature.

- **A destiny line from the Moon:** A destiny line from the Moon (Luna mount) indicates empathy and a constructive force for the inspiration and good of others.

- **Conscious observation:** Many learned discussions take place in the field of quantum physics regarding the impact of the observer on the observed. In his book *Seven Experiments That Could Change the World*, Rupert Sheldrake says "If the actual influence of the experimenters' mind is taken seriously, then many possibilities open up—even the possibility that the observer's mind may have psychokinetic powers. Perhaps 'mind over matter' phenomena take place in the microscopic realm of quantum physics."* Following in that same vein of thought, in *Holographic Universe*, author Michael

*Rupert Sheldrake, *Seven Experiments That Could Change the World* (New York: The Berkeley Publishing Group, 1995), 212.

Talbot suggests "that the observer influences the observed."* In this book we talk about changing the lines in our hands by drawing a copy of our hand, entering the changes we would like to see on our mounts and lines, and observing them consistently for about ten minutes, twice a day. Experiment for yourself and watch for the changes.

• **The "magnet pen":** The "magnet pen" was developed at the Palmistry Center with the aim of helping to stimulate the lines that we want to develop on our hands while at the same time working to erase worry or interference lines that may sap our energy. The magnet pen is based on the concept that the north pole, a positive charge, expands and the south pole, a negative charge, contracts, and that anything magnetic can impart these qualities. For example, a paper clip is not magnetic—it cannot attract another paper clip. However, if struck repeatedly with a magnet, the paper clip will become magnetized and will be able to pick up other paper clips. Similarly, the magnet pen enables us to magnetize our lines, which consequently speeds up our process of change—especially if, in correlation with the pen, we repeat positive affirmations as we imagine our lines as we would like them to be.

*Michael Talbot, *Holographic Universe* (New York: HarperCollins, 1991), 36–37.

Magnetic pen.

Index

Information found in figures or illustrations is denoted by an "f" following the page number.

Taking an Impression of Your Hands

The back pocket of this book contains one inked acetate sheet, sufficient for taking a print of each hand. Below are instructions for taking an impression of your hands. These prints will allow you to see details that may be difficult to discern from your actual palm. Use the information and the diagrams found in the book to determine your strengths and potential problem areas.

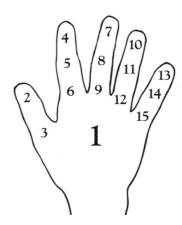

1. Prepare a large, clear surface (i.e., kitchen counter or table) and cover the area with newspaper. Have soap, paper towels, and a sink nearby for cleanup after taking prints. **Important:** For better clarity, *do not* wash hands before printing.

Remove wristwatch and any jewelry from hands and wrists, roll up long sleeves, and wear an apron or otherwise protect clothing.

2. Carefully separate the two layers of the inked acetate sheet. Place each layer down flat, inked sides up, on a section of newspaper. (Setting the sheets on a section of newspaper will provide enough surface "give" to ensure thorough hand-to-ink contact and give a complete print, including the center of the palm.) Place a blank sheet of paper next to the acetate sheets, also on top of a section of newspaper.

3. To take a print of each hand, begin with your right hand. Place your right palm down on one of the inked sheets, holding it still, yet relaxed and without any tension, to avoid smudging.

4. Use your left hand to press firmly down onto the parts of your right hand according to the numerical sequence shown in the diagram.

5. Use your left hand to hold down the edges of the acetate sheet, then lift your right hand in one clean motion. Place your inked, right hand down on the blank sheet of paper, hold your right hand still, and again press it with your left hand in the same numerical sequence as used earlier for inking.

When finished, use your left hand to hold down the edges of the paper and quickly lift up your right hand.

6. *Do not* wash your hands yet. You will want to complete the printing process and have a finished print of each hand, so tolerate ink on the back of one hand for a bit so as not to interfere with the printing process.

7. Now repeat the entire process using your left hand.

8. When done, clean up using more soap than water. With patience, all the ink will come off.

Now you have a print of each hand with which to consult the diagrams and information in the book regarding your own strengths and potential problem areas.